TOP 10 OF BRUSSELS, BRUGES, ANTWERP & GHENT

TOP 10 OF BRUSSELS, BRUGES, ANTWERP & GHENT

TOP 10 Highlights

The four great cities of northern Belgium share a rich cultural heritage dating back to medieval times, when this was one of the most vibrant trading regions in the world. Yet each is very different: Brussels is the business Capital of Europe, while Bruges is one of Europe's best preserved medieval cities. Ghent is a historic university city, while Antwerp still has the muscular stance of a great industrial centre. Each, in its own way, is richly rewarding – not only in cultural sights, but also in delightful and welcoming places to stay, eat and drink.

1 Grand Place, Brussels

For sheer architectural theatre, the historic centrepiece of Brussels is hard to beat – as it must have been three centuries ago *(see pp8–11)*.

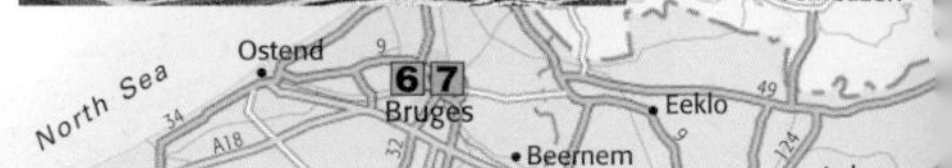

2 Musées Royaux des Beaux-Arts, Brussels

Brueghel, Rubens, Van Dyke, Magritte – this splendid collection takes the visitor on a tour of some of the greatest names in art *(see pp12–15)*.

3 Musée des Instruments de Musique, Brussels

Housed in a magnificent Art Nouveau building, the "mim" contains thousands of instruments – ancient, modern, ethnic and just plain wacky *(see pp16–17)*.

4 Musée Horta, Brussels

Victor Horta was the original Art Nouveau architect; his own house was the perfect expression of his art – down to the last doorknob. The building is now preserved as a shrine to Art Nouveau *(see pp18–19)*.

5 Centre Belge de la Bande Dessinée, Brussels

The "Comic Strip Centre" reveals all about this very Belgian art form: Tintin and beyond *(see pp20–21)*.

Preceding pages **Bruges: view from the Belfort on to the Rozenhoedkaai**

6 The Burg, Bruges

The old centre of Bruges is an architectural gem – a small, intimate square surrounded by historic buildings, each one offering something of fascination *(see pp22–3)*.

7 Groeningemuseum and Sint-Janshospitaal, Bruges

The great Flemish artists of the early 15th century, such as Hans Memling and Jan van Eyck, were among the first to perfect oil painting. These two collections demonstrate these artists' extraordinary skills, and show why they had such a profound influence on Italian art *(see pp24–5)*.

The Adoration of the Mystic Lamb, Ghent 8

This large, multi-panel altarpiece created in 1426–32 by Jan van Eyck and his brother Hubrecht remains one of the great cultural treasures of Europe *(see pp26–7)*.

9 Antwerp Cathedral

Antwerp's Cathedral of Our Lady is the city's main landmark, and the largest Gothic church in Belgium. Originating in the 14th century, its impressive interior is enhanced by two exceptional triptychs by Rubens: *The Raising of the Cross* and *The Descent from the Cross (see pp28–9)*.

10 Rubenshuis, Antwerp

Rubens' mansion has been carefully restored to show how it might have been when he lived here *(see pp30–31)*.

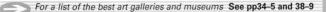

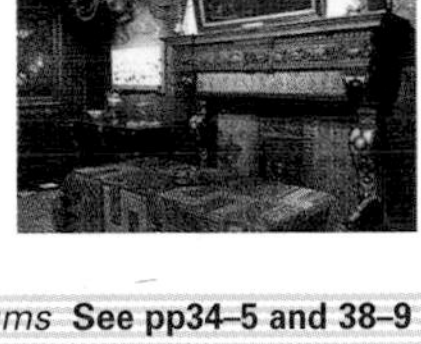

For a list of the best art galleries and museums **See pp34–5 and 38–9**

TOP 10 The Grand Place, Brussels

Brussels' Grand Place is the focal point of the city, a tirelessly uplifting masterpiece of unified architecture. Flanked by tightly packed rows of former guildhouses, bristling with symbolic sculpture and gilding, for many centuries this was the proud economic and administrative heart of the city. It was the setting for markets and fairs, pageants and jousts, for the proclamation of decrees, and public executions. Even without its old political and economic prestige and the bustle of through-traffic, it still throbs with animation.

Hôtel de Ville – detail of the façade

There are two famous bar-restaurants in the Grand Place – both pricey, but worth it for their utterly Bruxellois sense of style: Le Roy d'Espagne at No 1, and La Chaloupe d'Or at Nos 24–25.

A tourist office is located in the Hôtel de Ville and is a useful place to pick up information.

- *Map C3*
- *Hôtel de Ville: guided tours start 3pm Wed, 10am & 2pm Sun; arrive 15 minutes before. 02 548 04 47. Tour: €5*
- *Maison du Roi (Musée de la Ville de Bruxelles): open 10am–5pm Tue–Sun. 02 279 43 50. Admission: €4*
- *Musée du Cacao et du Chocolat (off the Grand Place): open 10am–4:30pm Tue–Sun. 02 514 20 48. Admission: €5.50*
- *Maison des Brasseurs (Musée de la Brasserie): open 10am–5pm daily. 02 511 49 87. Adm: €6*

Top 10 Sights

1. Hôtel de Ville
2. Maison du Roi
3. Le Renard
4. Le Cornet
5. The Tapis de Fleurs
6. Maison des Ducs de Brabant
7. Maison des Brasseurs
8. Le Cygne
9. Statue of Everard 't Serclaes
10. Maison des Boulangers

1 Hôtel de Ville

The Town Hall was the first major building on the Grand Place. Largely reconstructed since its 15th-century beginnings, it still has its original spire, topped by a statue of St Michael killing the devil.

2 Maison du Roi

This medieval-style "King's House" *(above)*, built in the 1870s, houses the Musée de la Ville de Bruxelles, a miscellany of city history, including costumes designed for the Manneken-Pis statue.

3 Le Renard

Like most of the buildings on the Grand Place, No 7 was a guildhouse *(gildehuizen)* – the prestigious headquarters of the Guild of Haberdashers. A striking gilded statue of a fox *(Le Renard)* sits above the door and illustrates the building's old name.

For more on the Manneken-Pis **See p10**

4 Le Cornet
This gloriously elaborate building (No 6) was once the guildhouse of the boatmen. Its marine adornments include a top storey resembling the stern of a galleon.

The Grand Place

7 Maison des Brasseurs
Called L'Arbre d'Or (the Golden Tree), the brewers' guildhouse (No 10) was designed by Guillaume de Bruyn. It is still used by the Confédération des Brasseries de Belgique, and contains a small museum of brewing.

8 Le Cygne
"The Swan" (No 9) was rebuilt as a private residence in 1698, but in 1720 it was acquired by the Guild of Butchers. It later became a café, and Karl Marx held meetings of the German Workers' Party here.

10 Maison des Boulangers
The bakers' guildhouse *(above)* is coated with symbols, including six figures representing the essential elements of breadmaking. The unusual octagonal lantern on the roof is topped by a striking gilded statue of Fame.

5 The Tapis de Fleurs
Every even-numbered year for five days in mid-August, the Grand Place is taken over by a massive floral display known as the Carpet of Flowers *(above)*.

6 Maison des Ducs de Brabant
The south-eastern flank of this impressive Neo-Classical building was conceived (in 1698) as a single block of seven units by Guillaume de Bruyn.

9 Statue of Everard 't Serclaes
Everard 't Serclaes died on this site in 1388 resisting Flemish occupation. Passers-by stroke the limbs of his bronze statue *(below)* for luck.

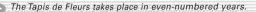

Not quite the real thing
The guildhouses of the Grand Place are built largely in the Flemish Renaissance style of the late 16th and early 17th centuries. Little of it actually dates from this period, however. On 13–14 August 1695, under the orders of Louis XIV, French troops led by Marshal de Villeroy lined up their cannons, took aim at the spire of the Hôtel de Ville, and pulverized the city centre. In defiance, the citizens set about reconstructing the Grand Place, a task completed in just five years.

The Tapis de Fleurs takes place in even-numbered years.

Left **La Bourse** Centre **Église Saint-Nicolas** Right **Rue des Bouchers**

TOP 10 Around the Grand Place

1 Manneken-Pis

No one knows why this tiny bronze statue of a boy peeing a jet of water has become such a cherished symbol of Brussels, but it has. Since the early 18th century, costumes of all kinds have been made for him; he now has over 800. *corner of Rue de l'Étuve and Rue du Chêne • Map B3*

2 Galeries Royales de Saint-Hubert

Built in 1847, this was the first shopping arcade in Europe, and boasts magnificent vaulted glass ceilings. *Map C2*

3 Rues des Bouchers

Many of the streets around the Grand Place reflect the trades that once operated there. The "Street of the Butchers" and its intersecting Petite Rue des Bouchers are famous for their lively restaurants and colourful displays of food. *Map C3*

Galeries Royales de Saint-Hubert

4 Église Saint-Nicolas

St Nicholas of Myra – a.k.a. Santa Claus – was the patron saint of merchants, and this church has served the traders of the Grand Place and surrounds since the 14th century. Its interior has retained an impressively medieval atmosphere, despite desecration by Protestant rebels in the 16th century, damage during the bombardment of 1695, and rebuilding in the 1950s. *Rue au Beurre 1 • Map C3 • 02 513 80 22 • Open 8am–6:30pm Mon–Fri, 9am–6pm Sat, 9am–7:30pm Sun • Free*

5 La Bourse

The Stock Exchange is an unmistakable feature of the Brussels landscape. Built in 1873 like a Greek temple and lavishly decorated, it is now used by Euronext (European stock markets) and functions as an occasional exhibition space. Beneath it are the exposed archaeological remains of a convent founded in 1238, known as Bruxella 1238. *Map B3 • Bruxella 1238: 02 279 43 55. Guided tours first Wed of month (10:15am for tours in English; departs from outside Maison du Roi on the Grand Place)*

6 Musée du Costume et de la Dentelle

This small but surprisingly rewarding museum dedicated to historic costume and lace has a limited but choice selection of exhibits. *Rue de la Violette 12 • Map C3 • 02 213 44 50 • Open 10am–5pm Thu–Tue • Adm charge*

For the very few recommended restaurants in and around the Rue des Bouchers **See p74**

7 Biscuiterie Dandoy

Brussels' best makers of biscuits (cookies) have been perfecting their craft since 1829. Behind a ravishing shop window lie goodies such as *speculoos*, *sablés* and waffles. *Rue au Beurre 31 • Map C3*

8 Église Notre-Dame de Bon Secours

The most striking feature of this delightful church, built in 1664–94, is its soaring hexagonal choir, rising to a domed ceiling. The façade bears the coat of arms of the enlightened 18th-century governor of the Austrian Netherlands, Charles of Lorraine. *Rue du Marché au Charbon 91 • Map B3 • 02 514 31 13 • Open daily Jun–Nov: 9:30am–6pm, Dec–May: 10am–5pm • Free*

Wedding dress, Musée du Costume

9 Place Saint-Géry

The square that marks the site of Brussels' first settlement is today dominated by Les Halles de Saint-Géry, an attractive iron and red-brick structure built in 1881 as a meat market. Now a craft market, exhibition space and café, it is the central focus of an area known increasingly for its nightlife. *Map B3*

10 Statue of Charles Buls

In Place Agora is one of Brussels' most delightful statues: a portrait of the splendidly bearded and moustachioed artist, scholar and reformer Charles Buls (1837–1914) and his dog. Buls, who served as Burgomaster from 1891 to 1899, is credited with restoring the Grand Place. *Map C3*

The Île Saint-Géry and the River Senne

Brussels began as a group of little islands on a marshy river. Legend has it that in the 6th century AD, St Géry, Bishop of Cambrai, founded a church on one of these islands, and a settlement grew around it. The name Broeksele (later Brussels), meaning "house in the swamp", is first mentioned in 966, and a castle was built on the island by Charles, Duke of Lorraine, a decade later, effectively launching the city. There was a chapel on the island until 1798, when it was finally destroyed by occupying French revolutionary forces. The river, called the Senne, ran through the city until the 19th century, approximately along the line between the Gare du Midi and the Gare du Nord. Never large, it became overwhelmed by the growing population, and such a health hazard that following another outbreak of cholera, it was covered over in 1867–71. This process created the Boulevard Anspach and the Boulevard Adolphe Max, among others, while the river formed part of the city's new sewer and drainage system. It can still be glimpsed here and there in the city.

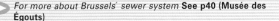

***The River Senne* by Jean-Baptiste van Moer**

For more about Brussels' sewer system **See p40 (Musée des Égouts)**

TOP 10 Musées Royaux des Beaux-Arts

Brussels' "Royal Museums of the Fine Arts" are a tour de force. *Many of the greatest names in art history are represented here – remarkably, they are predominantly home-grown. The museums are divided into three closely integrated parts, the Musée d'Art Ancien (15th to 18th centuries), the Musée Fin-de-Siècle (19th and early 20th centuries) and the Musée Magritte. The museums are undergoing a major renovation, which means that some exhibits might have been moved, check the website for more information before you go.*

Musées Royaux des Beaux-Arts, façade

The Museums have their own good cafeteria. Far more exciting, however, is, mim on top of the nearby Musée des Instruments de Musique ***(see pp16–17)*****; and just a short walk away are the cafés of the Place du Grand Sablon, including the exquisite** ***chocolatier*** **Wittamer** ***(see p72)*****.**

The Museums may be quieter mid-week during the middle of the day so this can be a good time for a more leisurely visit.

• Rue de la Régence 3 • Map C4 • 02 508 32 11 • www.fine-arts-museum.be • Open 9am–5pm Tue–Sun • Admission €13, including entry to the Magritte Museum; otherwise, €8 (€2 for 6–25 yrs, under 6s free). Free admission on 1st Wed of each month after 1pm

Top 10 Works

1. The Justice of Othon
2. Lamentation
3. The Fall of Icarus
4. The Martyrdom of St Livincus
5. The Death of Marat
6. Portrait of Antony of Burgundy
7. The Martyrdom of St Sebastian
8. The King Drinks
9. Four Studies of the Head of a Moor
10. The Domain of Arnheim

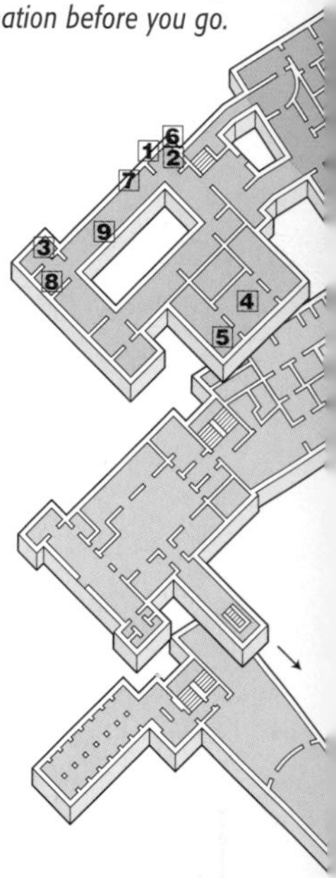

1 The Justice of Othon

This snapshot of brutal medieval life painted by Dirk Bouts (c.1420–75) in 1471–73, is a tale told in two panels – a kind of early comic strip. With brilliant clarity and detail, it depicts how Emperor Othon (Otto II) was fooled by his wife into beheading an innocent man for adultery.

2 Lamentation

Rogier van der Weyden was known for the disturbing emotional charge of his work, as in this painting of c.1420–50 of the crucified Christ in his mother's arms *(right)*.

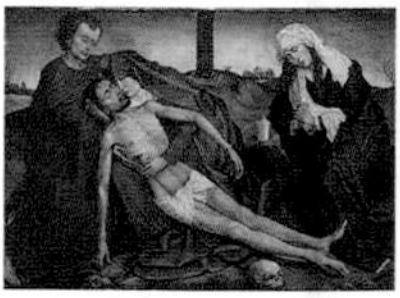

3 The Fall of Icarus

This work of 1567 *(above)* by Pieter Brueghel the Elder wryly upstages the drama with prettified normality.

4 The Martyrdom of St Livincus

At his best, Rubens created works of staggering dynamism, compelling the eye to move through the painting, and inspiring a sense of exhilaration and awe. The savagery of this depiction of cruel martyrdom also conveys the power of redemption.

For more about the most famous Belgian artists **See pp36–37**

5 The Death of Marat

The French revolutionary Marat was murdered in his bath by a female assassin. This portrait *(right)* by Jacques-Louis David is strikingly realistic.

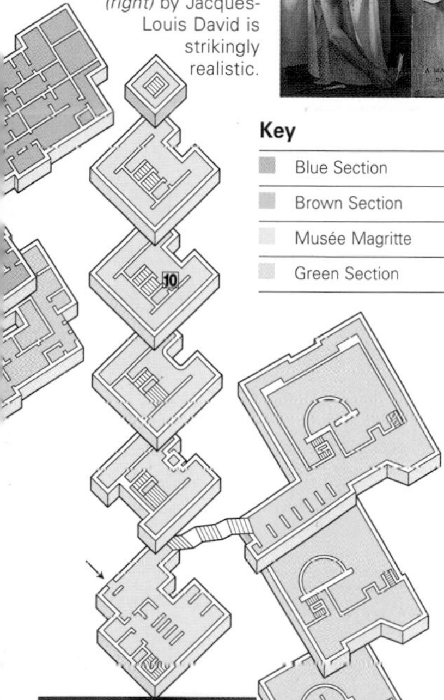

Key

■	Blue Section
■	Brown Section
■	Musée Magritte
■	Green Section

8 The King Drinks

Flemish Baroque artist Jacques Jordaens perfectly captures the muscular joviality of a feast at Epiphany in his painting of 1640.

9 Four Studies of the Head of a Moor

This quadruplet of sketches (c. 1640) shows Peter Paul Rubens' attempts to capture the exotic nature of his subject. The same sketch also appears in his Adoration of the Magi (1609).

10 The Domain of Arnheim

René Magritte poses visual conundrums. In this painting of 1962 *(below)*, ambiguous feelings of threat and protection are suggested simultaneously.

6 Portrait of Antony of Burgundy

Flemish artist Rogier van der Weyden painted this portrait *(above)* of the illegitimate child of Philip the Good (c. 1460). The arrow indicates his membership of the Archers' Guild.

7 The Martyrdom of St Sebastian

Hans Memling's painting (c. 1475) depicts St Sebastian's untimely end *(below)*. The saint was shot to death by royal archers for converting to Christianity.

Gallery Guide

The museums' collections are arranged by centuries, each with its own colour code. The Blue Section is currently closed for renovation, so all art works from the 15th–18th centuries are on display in the Brown Section. Musée Magritte houses the largest collection of the artist's work, including paintings, photographs and drawings, while the descending levels (-3 to -8) of the Green Section exhibit 19th- and 20th-century art to the present day.

For more on the Belgian Symbolists **See p15**

Left **Main entrance hall** Centre ***La Belle Captive*, Magritte** Right **View of main galleries**

TOP 10 Beaux-Arts: Features and Collections

1 The Buildings

Set on the crest of the Coudenberg, the old royal enclave of Brussels, the museum's main buildings were designed by one of the leading architects of the day, Alphonse Balat (1818–95). He is also famous for designing the royal greenhouses at Laeken *(see p80)* and for having taught Victor Horta *(see pp18–19)*.

2 Renaissance/Flemish Primitives (Blue Section)

The earliest rooms contain enough 15th- and 16th-century work for an entire visit. The creations of the early Flemish oil painters (the so-called "Primitives") show the influence of the medieval manuscript illuminators; later works reveal the increasing influence of the Italian Renaissance.

3 The Brueghel Collection

The Blue Section also includes the world's second largest collection of work by Pieter Brueghel the Elder, which hang alongside paintings by his son Pieter Brueghel the Younger, many of which were copied from his father's work.

4 Golden Age/17th Century (Brown Section)

Flemish painting had its second golden age in the 17th century, with such figures as Rubens, Jordaens and Van Dyck. This section shows why Antwerp was a key centre of European art in this period.

5 The Rubens Collection

Part of the Brown Section, the Rubens Collection shows why this painter was so fêted. To those who think of Rubens only in terms of scenes filled with plump, pink, naked ladies, this collection comes as a revelation, displaying vigour, spontaneity and artistic risk-taking.

6 Realism (Musée Fin-de-Siècle)

The second half of the 19th century was plagued by political and social upheaval. A number of artists reacted to this unrest by establishing the Société Libre des Beaux-Arts in Brussels in 1868 to create art promoting freedom, sincerity and nature. Félicien Rops and Emile Wauters were among them.

7 Belgian Impressionism (Musée Fin-de-Siècle)

Characterised by the works of James Ensor, Henri de Braekeleer and members of Les XX (a group of twenty Belgian painters, designers and sculptors who held annual shows), this 1880s genre played with light, shade and realistic landscapes.

8 Gillion Crowet Collection (Musée Fin-de-Siècle)

This outstanding collection showcases the work of Art Nouveau masters such as Victor Horta, Émile Gallé, Alphonse Mucha and Fernand Khnopff.

The Musées Royaux des Beaux-Arts are undergoing major renovations, so some exhibits may change.

9 Magritte Museum

The work of René Magritte is so often seen in reproduction that it may come as a surprise to see it up close. The impressive museum, in a separate section of the Musées Royaux des Beaux-Arts, houses the world's largest collection of his work *(see below)*.

Le Ruisseau **by Léon Frédéric (1856–1940)**

10 Symbolism (Musée Fin-de-Siècle)

Symbolism sought to move away from the materialism of Impressionism and explore dreams, tears and the soul. Works by Jean Delville, Léon Frédéric and Émile Fabry represent the movement.

René Magritte

René Magritte (1898–1967) began drawing at the age of 12 and went on to train at the Académie Royale des Beaux-Arts in Brussels. His life was forever changed when his mother committed suicide by drowning herself when he was just 14 years old. It is said that he was present when his mother's body was dredged from the River Sambre and the sight of her dress covering her face haunted his early paintings. In 1922, Magritte married artist and photographer Georgette Berger. Magritte's first exhibition in 1927 was critically panned and smarting from the failure, he moved to Paris. Here he met André Breton, one of the founders of the Surrealist movement. Magritte stayed in Paris for three years, before returning to his career in advertising in German-occupied Brussels. He returned to painting after World War II and became renowned for his quirky, question-provoking Surrealist art. Magritte died in Brussels in 1967.

Georgette and René Magritte

Top 10 Magritte Paintings

1. *The Treachery of Images (This Continues to Not Be a Pipe)* (1952)
2. *Black Magic* (1945)
3. *The Return* (1940)
4. *Treasure Island* (1942)
5. *Georgette* (1937)
6. *The Unexpected Answer* (1933)
7. *Man from the Sea* (1927)
8. *Discovery* (1927)
9. *The Secret Player* (1927)
10. *The Domain of Arnheim* (1962) *(see p13)*

Musée des Instruments de Musique

The Musée des Instruments de Musique, often referred to as "Le mim", has a supreme collection of musical instruments from ancient to modern. The exhibits – selected from a collection totalling more than 9,000 pieces – have been beautifully arranged, and headphones permit visitors to hear what the instruments actually sound like. Added to this, the museum is housed in an exhilarating location: the classic Art Nouveau department store called "Old England". When you need refreshment, you can go up to the Restaurant mim on the top floor, which has one of the best views over Brussels.

The "Old England" building housing "Le mim"

mim Restaurant, on the top floor of the museum, serves refreshments of all kinds, plus reasonably-priced light lunch dishes such as sandwiches, pasta and a selection of salads. If this is too busy, you can always head off for the cafés of the Place du Grand Sablon, just a short walk away.

Expect to spend at least two hours in this museum; to do it full justice, give it three to four hours. Note that although the Museum officially closes at 5pm, staff like to empty the exhibition rooms by 4:45pm.

- *Rue Montagne de la Cour 2*
- *Map D4*
- *02 545 01 30*
- *www.mim.be*
- *Open 9:30am–5pm Tue–Thu, 10am–5pm Sat–Sun*
- *Admission: €8 (free on first Wed of month)*

Top 10 Features

1. The "Old England" Building
2. Visitor Guidance System
3. 20th-century Instruments
4. Mechanical Instruments
5. Non-European Instruments
6. Stringed Instruments
7. The Historical Survey
8. mim Restaurant
9. European Folk Instruments
10. Keyboard Instruments

1 The "Old England" Building

Completed in 1899, this is a classic example of the innovative iron-and-glass structures produced by Art Nouveau architects. When visiting the mim, make sure to look at the interior of the museum itself.

2 Visitor Guidance System

A visitor guidance system, similar to an iPod Touch, is issued to all ticket holders; as you approach selected exhibits, recordings of those instruments are triggered with accompanying photographs.

3 20th-century Instruments

Technology has had a major impact on music in the late 20th century, from electric amplification to synthesizers and computer-generated music. This small collection offers a fascinating snapshot. If you don't know what an *ondes martenot* is, here's your chance to find out.

4 Mechanical Instruments

The ingenuity of instrument-makers is evident in this collection, which includes some outrageously elaborate musical boxes and a *carillon* – a set of bells used to play tunes.

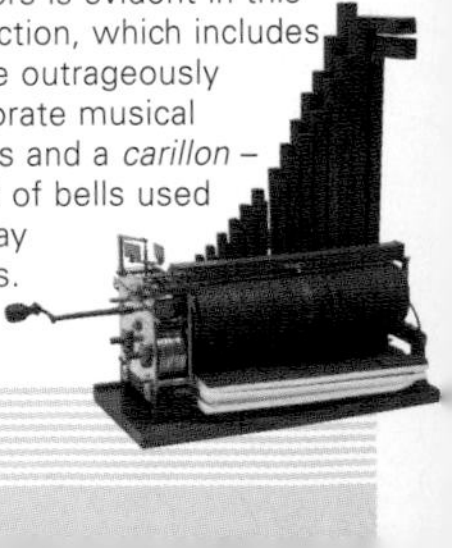

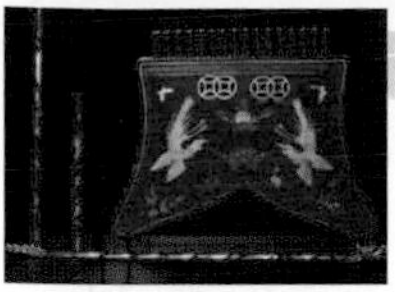

5 Non-European Instruments

The mim runs a strong line in ethnomusicology. This impressive collection includes panpipes, sitars, African harps and drums, gamelan orchestras, and giant Tibetan horns.

8 mim Restaurant

Even if you don't need refuelling, take the lift up to the 10th floor to admire the view. From here you can see the statue of St Michael glistening on the top of the spire of the Hôtel de Ville in the Grand Place, and far across town to the Basilique Nationale and the Atomium.

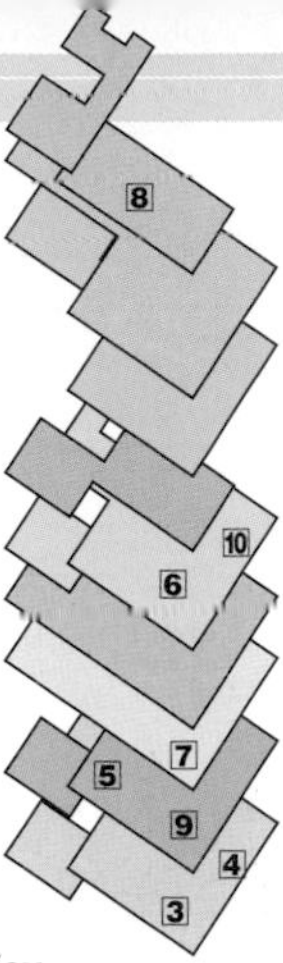

Key

- Basement (-1)
- First floor
- Second floor
- Third Floor
- Fourth floor
- Fifth floor
- Seventh floor
- Eighth floor
- Tenth floor

6 Stringed Instruments

Sharing the 2nd floor is the stringed instrument section, including violins of all shapes and sizes, psalteries, dulcimers, harps, lutes and guitars. There is also a reconstruction of a violin-maker's workshop.

7 The Historical Survey

This section charts the evolution of western "art" instruments from antiquity through the Renaissance to the 19th century. The headphone guide shows the evolving complexity of musical sound.

9 European Folk Instruments

This fascinating collection includes pipes, rattles, accordions, hurdy-gurdies and some splendid oddities – chief among them a collection of Belgian glass trumpets.

10 Keyboard Instruments

Star exhibits include harpsichords by the Ruckers family *(below)*, who worked in Antwerp from the 16th century.

Museum Guide

The museum is set out on four of the building's ten floors. Floor –1 is devoted to mechanical and 20th-century instruments. The first floor covers folk instruments. The historical survey of western musical instruments begins on the 2nd floor and continues on the 4th floor, where the keyboard and stringed instruments are concentrated. There is a shop on the 3rd floor, library (access by appointment) on the 5th and a concert hall on the 8th; the restaurant is on the top floor. The floors are connected by stairs and a lift.

For more on Art Nouveau architecture in Brussels
See pp44–5

TOP 10 Musée Horta, Brussels

In the late 19th century, Brussels was a centre for avant-garde design, and a rapidly growing city. To feed the market for stylish mansions, architects scavenged history for ideas; the result was the so-called "eclectic style". In 1893, the gifted architect Victor Horta created a totally new style – later labelled "Art Nouveau" – full of sensuous curves and artistic surprises, elaborated with wrought iron, stained glass, mosaics, murals and finely crafted woodwork. Horta brought this style to full maturity when he built his own house – now the Musée Horta.

The Salon, Musée Horta

There are several interesting bars and cafés nearby, around Place du Châtelain. For a spot of good-value lunch before the museum's 2pm opening hour, try the charming La Canne en Ville *(see p81)*; for somewhere with real design flair, head for the extraordinary Quincaillerie, which dates from 1903 *(see p81)*.

The Musée Horta is at the heart of a cluster of Art Nouveau buildings. Key streets include Rue Defacqz, Rue Faider and Rue Paul-Émile Janson. Hôtel Hannon is also close by *(see pp44–5)*.

- *Rue Américaine 25, Brussels 1060 (Saint-Gilles)*
- *Map G2*
- *02 543 04 90*
- *www.hortamuseum.be*
- *Open 2–5:30pm Tue–Sun. Closed Mon, public hols*
- *Admission: €7*

Top 10 Features

1. The Building
2. The Staircase
3. Structural Ironwork
4. Fixtures and Fittings
5. Furniture
6. Leaded Glass
7. Mosaics
8. Woodwork
9. Art Nouveau Sculpture Collection
10. Scale Model of the Maison du Peuple

1 The Building

When designing for his clients, Horta liked to tailor the house according to how they lived. His own house has two distinct parts: on the left (from the outside), his residence; on the right, his offices and studio.

2 The Staircase

The interior design hangs on a central stairwell, lit from the top by a large, curving skylight. The ironwork bannisters have been given a typically exuberant flourish *(above)*.

3 Structural Ironwork

In what was considered a bold gesture at the time, Horta used iron structures to support his houses. He even made a virtue of it, by leaving some of the iron exposed and drawing attention to it with wrought-iron embellishments *(below)*.

For more of Horta's Art Nouveau buildings **See pp44–5**

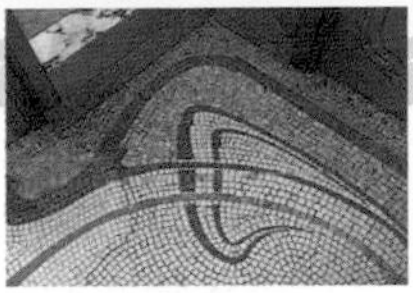

4 Fixtures and Fittings

Horta was an *ensemblier*: he liked to design an entire building in all its detail, down to the last light fixture, door handle and coat hook. This attention to detail conveys the impression of complete architectural mastery: nothing is left to chance.

7 Mosaics

The sinuous lines of Art Nouveau design in the mosaic tiling of the dining room floor *(above)* help to soften the effect of the white-enamelled industrial brick lining the walls.

9 Art Nouveau Sculpture Collection

Throughout the museum are several fine sculptures by late 19th-century Belgian artists. Look out for *La Ronde des Heures (below)*, in the rear salon on the first floor. This intriguing little bronze was created by Philippe Wolfers (1858–1929), a leading Art Nouveau jeweller and silversmith who worked with Horta.

10 Scale Model of the Maison du Peuple

Although few have survived, Horta was well-known for his designs for commercial and public buildings. The Maison du Peuple was an innovative cast-iron structure built for the Société Coopérative in 1895. A scale model of it can be seen in the cellar.

5 Furniture

In addition to door handles and coat hooks, Horta also liked to design the furniture to go in his houses. Although it bears a definite Art Nouveau stamp, Horta's furniture tends to be simple, restrained and practical.

6 Leaded Glass

The nature of leaded glass – glass shapes held together by lead strips – stimulated the artistic flair of Art Nouveau architects. It appears at various points in the house – notably the door panels and stairwell skylight.

8 Woodwork

There is a note of austerity as well as luxury in Art Nouveau design. The richly carved wood in the dining room is left natural, allowing the quality of the wood to speak for itself *(below)*.

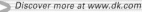

Victor Horta

The son of a Ghent shoemaker, Victor Horta (1861–1947) studied architecture from the age of 13. After designing the Hôtel Tassel *(see page 44)* in 1893, his reputation soared. Thereafter he designed houses, department stores and public buildings. With World War I, Art Nouveau fell from favour, and Horta turned to a harder style, seen in his Palais des Beaux-Arts in Brussels. He was awarded the title of Baron in 1932.

TOP 10 Centre Belge de la Bande Dessinée

We've all heard of Tintin – perhaps the most famous Belgian in the world. But this comic-strip hero is just one of hundreds produced in Belgium over the last century. The comic strip – bande dessinée *in French – is called the "ninth art". The library at Brussels' Centre Belge de la Bande Dessinée contains 40,000 volumes – it's taken* that *seriously. Set out in a renovated fabric warehouse, the CBBD (pronounced cébébédé) presents the history of the form, shows how strips are made, and explores some of the key characters and their creators.*

Brasserie Horta

The CBBD's own Brasserie Horta is a convenient place for refreshments, and serves a good range of lunch dishes. If that doesn't appeal, you are only a short walk from the Grand Place and its multitude of cafés and restaurants. Nearer at hand is the famous bar A la Mort Subite *(see p72)*, a traditional place to sample *gueuze* beer.

Note that the CBBD is *not* guaranteed to entertain small children, especially if they do not speak French or Dutch. It is, rather, a museum showing the evolution of the craft. There are free guides in English.

- *Rue des Sables 20*
- *Map D2*
- *02 219 19 80* • *www.comicscenter.net*
- *Open 10am–6pm Tue–Sun*
- *Admission: €8*

Top 10 Features

1. The Building
2. Invention of the Comic Strip
3. The Art of the Comic Strip
4. The Gallery
5. Library
6. Temporary Exhibitions
7. The Belgian Comic Strip Movement
8. Slumberland Bookshop
9. Horta and the Waucquez Warehouse
10. Tintin

1 The Building

The CBBD occupies what was formerly the Magasins Waucquez, an innovative Art Nouveau structure of cast iron supporting large expanses of glass, designed by Victor Horta in 1903–6 *(main image) (see p45).*

2 Invention of the Comic Strip

This exhibition explores how the comic strip began. Discover the history of the art form and its use by civilizations throughout the world – from early cave art to 19th-century magazines.

3 The Art of the Comic Strip

This exhibition contains a selection of original drawings showing how comic strips are made. A wide range of artists, from the traditional to the modern, donated their sketches and studies to show each step involved in the process of creating a comic strip.

4 The Gallery

The Gallery displays a broad range of international albums – both classical and contemporary style. The space is dedicated to new comics from a wide variety of genres from fantasy and satire, to crime and autobiography.

8 Slumberland Bookshop

Named after the Little Nemo adventure, the shop stocks everything on the comic strip theme.

5 Library

The library *(above)* has a public reading room, which is open to anyone with a museum ticket.

9 Horta and the Waucquez Warehouse

The exhibition covers the history of this Art Nouveau warehouse.

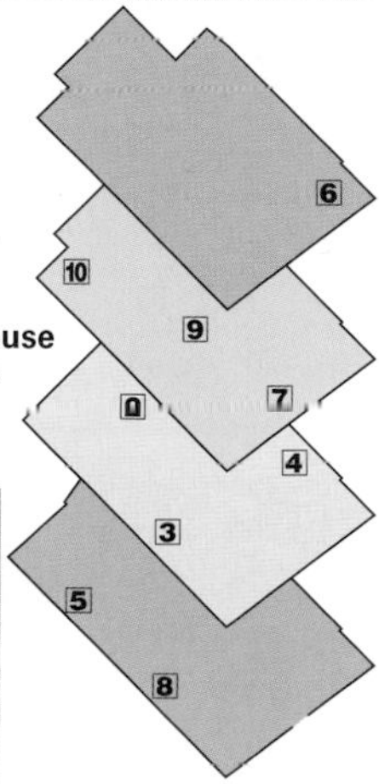

Museum floorplan

Key

- Ground floor
- First floor
- Second floor
- Third floor

6 Temporary Exhibitions

A constantly changing space used for exhibitions dedicated to a particular artist, theme or movement within comic strips.

7 The Belgian Comic Strip Movement

The two major movements of Belgian comic strip art – the Brussels and the Marcinelle genres – are explored here.

10 Tintin

Of course, the main hero of the CBBD is the famous boy-reporter Tintin *(above)*, creation of Hergé. Translated into some 40 languages, over 140 million copies of the books have been sold worldwide. The museum acknowledges his status with 3-D models of key characters, and the rocket that went to the moon.

Tintin

The story of Tintin goes back to 1929, when he first appeared in a children's newspaper supplement *Le Petit Vingtième*. His Brussels-born inventor Hergé (Georges Rémi, *see p48*) developed the character as he took him through a series of adventures related to real events, such as the rise of fascism *(King Ottakar's Sceptre)*. The enduring charm of Tintin is his naive determination, as well as the multitude of archetypal characters that surround him, such as Captain Haddock, Professor Calculus and, of course, Tintin's faithful dog Snowy.

For more about Hergé **See p48**

TOP 10 The Burg, Bruges

Bruges began life in the 10th century as a castle built on marshland formed by the River Reie. The castle has disappeared, but the charming square that replaced it, the Burg, has remained the historic heart of the city over the centuries. The most impressive building is the Stadhuis, a classic late-medieval town hall built when Bruges was a hub of international trade. Just about every century is represented by the buildings on the Burg, and visiting them discloses many of the fascinating secrets that lie behind this extraordinary city.

Breidelstraat

De Garre *(see p91)*, just off the Burg, is an ancient café serving drinks and snacks.

All the sights in the Burg are high in quality but small in content. You can see everything in an hour or two.

- *Map L4*
- *Heilig Bloedbasiliek/ St Basil's Chapel: Burg 10. Open Apr–mid-Oct: 9:30am–noon & 2–5pm daily; mid-Oct–Mar: 10am–noon & 2–5pm Mon, Tue & Thu–Sun. Admission to Schatkamer (museum): €1.50*
- *Stadhuis ("Gothic Hall"): Burg 12. Open 9:30am–5pm daily. Admission: €4 (inc. audioguide and entrance to Renaissancezaal; children under 12 free)*
- *Renaissancezaal van het Brugse Vrije: Burg 11a. Open 9:30am–12:30pm & 1:30–5pm daily. Admission: included in admission price for Stadhuis*

Top 10 Sights

1. Breidelstraat
2. Heilig Bloedbasiliek
3. St Basil's Chapel
4. Stadhuis
5. Oude Civiele Griffie
6. Renaissancezaal van het Brugse Vrije
7. Landhuis van het Brugse Vrije
8. The North Side
9. Proostdij
10. Blinde Ezelstraat

1 Breidelstraat

The quaint little street *(above left)* that connects Bruges' main market place, the Markt, to the Burg is lined with shops selling souvenirs as well as one of the city's most famous products, lace.

2 Heilig Bloedbasiliek

On the west side of the Burg lies the Basilica of the Holy Blood *(above)*, a chapel lavishly restored in Neo-Gothic style in the late 19th century. Its tiny museum holds its most famous relic, a phial of blood said to be Christ's.

3 St Basil's Chapel

Beneath the Heilig Bloedbasiliek is another chapel of an utterly contrasting mood *(below)*. Constructed of hefty grey stone in the 12th century, it is a superb and atmospheric example of muscular Romanesque style, and a reminder of the Burg's origins as a castle.

For more on Bruges' famous festival, the Heilig Bloedprocessie **See p50**

4 Stadhuis

One of medieval Europe's great secular buildings *(main image)*, the Stadhuis (town hall) is a magnificent expression of Bruges' self-confidence in medieval times, built in 1376–1420 in aptly named Flamboyant Gothic style. It was much restored in the late 19th century.

7 Landhuis van het Brugse Vrije

This sober 18th-century mansion was the head-quarters of the "Liberty of Bruges", which was an administrative jurisdiction covering a large region around the city, while Bruges governed itself separately.

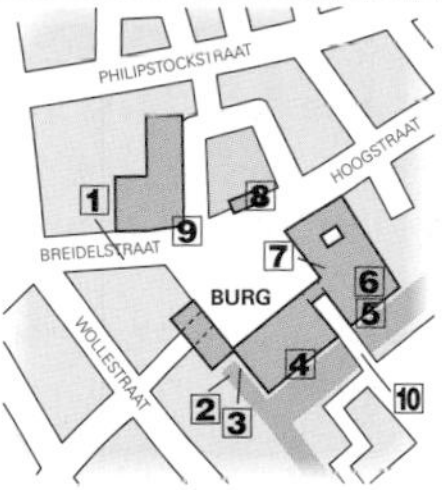

Plan of the Burg

10 Blinde Ezelstraat

A picturesque street leads off from the south of the Burg, beneath the arch that links the Oude Griffie to the Stadhuis. The name "Blind Donkey St" may relate to a nearby inn famed for its cheap beer.

5 Oude Civiele Griffie

The Renaissance touched Bruges' archi-tecture only lightly; this "Old Recorders' House", built in 1534–7 *(below)*, is the exception.

6 Renaissancezaal van het Brugse Vrije

In the corner of the Burg is the Renaissance Room, whose star exhibit is the Charles V Chimneypiece, a virtuoso piece of 16th-century wood carving.

8 The North Side

This ultra-modern Pavilion *(above)* by Toyo Ito was built in 2002 on the site of the "missing" cathedral *(see panel)*, to mark Bruges' year as a Cultural Capital of Europe.

9 Proostdij

The Provost's House lining the north side of the Burg is in Flemish Baroque style (1622), with a roof-line balustrade topped by the figure of Justice.

The Missing Cathedral

Images of the centre of Bruges before 1799 show the north side of the Burg occupied by the impressive hulk of the Sint-Donaaskerk. The first church on this site dated back to Bruges' origins, and Jan van Eyck was buried here. Gradually enlarged over the centuries, in 1559 it became the city's cathe-dral. But during the occupation by French revolutionary forces, it was demolished. Excavated parts of its foundations can still be seen in the Crowne Plaza Hotel *(see p127)*.

For more on Emperor Charles V **See p46**

Two Museums of Bruges

These two museums contain some of the world's finest examples of late medieval art, presenting a treasured selection of work by artists such as Jan van Eyck (c.1390–1441) and Hans Memling (c.1440–94). The two museums are on separate sites, a short distance apart. The Groeningemuseum is a small and charming gallery with a radical edge. The Sint-Janshospitaal is part of the medieval hospital that commissioned Memling's paintings for the very chapel in which they can still be seen.

Façade of the Groeningemuseum

The Groeningemuseum is only a short walk from the centre of town, where there is a wide choice of cafés and restaurants *(see p91).*

Available from the tourist office, the Bruges City Card (€33 for 48 hours or €43 for 72 hours) gives access to 24 museums (including the two on these pages), a canal trip, a bus tour and other discounts. Visit www.bruggecitycard.be for more details.

• Groeningemuseum: Dijver 12. Map L4. 050 44 87 11. Open 9:30am–5pm Tue–Sun. Admission: €8 (children under 12 free)
• Sint-Janshospitaal: Mariastraat 38. Map K5. Open 9:30am–5pm Tue–Sun. Admission: €8 (children under 12 free)

Top 10 Paintings

1. The Last Judgment
2. The Judgment of Cambyses
3. The St Ursula Shrine
4. The Legend of St Ursula
5. The Moreel Triptych
6. Secret-Reflet
7. Madonna with Canon Joris van der Paele
8. The Invention of the Art of Drawing
9. The Triptych with Sts John the Baptist and John the Evangelist
10. The Adoration of the Magi

1 The Last Judgment

Hieronymus Bosch (c.1450–1516) is famous for his nightmarish paintings of spiritual anguish, torture and hell. This example *(above)* is a perplexing insight into the religious psyche of the times.

2 The Judgment of Cambyses

In 1488, Bruges ill-advisedly imprisoned Philip the Fair, Duke of Burgundy. This large diptych by Gerard David depicting the gruesome flaying of a corrupt judge *(right)* was commissioned for the town hall as a sort of public apology.

3 The St Ursula Shrine

Completed by Hans Memling in 1479, this metre-long reliquary *(above)* depicts the Legend of St Ursula in six exquisitely detailed panels.

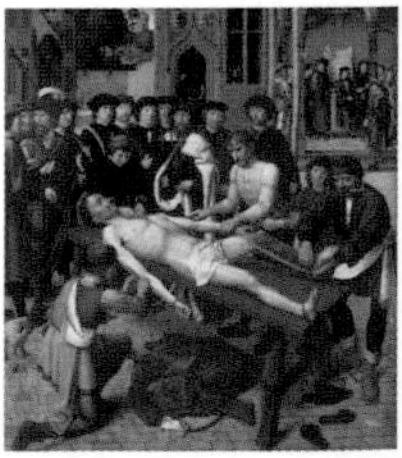

4 The Legend of St Ursula

This series of panels by the "Master of the Saint Ursula Legend" tells the popular medieval tale of St Ursula and her company of 11,000 virgins, cruelly martyred in pagan Germany.

6 Secret-Reflet

This Symbolist work *(right)* of 1902 by Belgian painter Fernand Khnopff (1858–1921) includes an image of the Sint-Janshospitaal. The title refers to the play on the word "reflection" in the two images.

7 Madonna with Canon Joris van der Paele

The supreme masterpiece of the collection *(above)* was painted in 1436 by Jan van Eyck. The detail is astonishing.

8 The Invention of the Art of Drawing

This Neo-Classical masterpiece, by Joseph Benôit Suvée (1971), is one of the Groeninge's most prized possessions. The painting depicts the daughter of Greek potter, Butades, drawing the silhouette of her lover.

10 The Adoration of the Magi

This work, displayed in the Sint-Janshospitaal's chapel, was painted by Memling in 1479. It is known as the Jan Floreins Triptych after the patron, seen kneeling behind a low wall on the left of the central panel *(below)*.

The Golden Age of Bruges

Under the dukes of Burgundy Bruges prospered, and in 1429 it became the capital of the Burgundian empire. Its elite became wealthy, educated patrons of the arts. The dukes of Burgundy married into European royalty: Philip the Good married Isabella of Portugal; Charles the Bold, Margaret of York. Their marriages were celebrated with vast feasts – the stuff of European legends. This is the world glimpsed in the paintings of the Flemish masters.

5 The Moreel Triptych

Willem Moreel, the burgomaster of Bruges, commissioned this work *(above)* from Hans Memling in 1484. Moreel is depicted in the left-hand panel, his wife in the right.

9 The Triptych with Sts John the Baptist and John the Evangelist

Painted by Memling in 1479, this work celebrates the two St Johns, patron saints of the Sint-Janshospitaal.

For Jacob van Oost's *Portrait of a Bruges Family* **See p84**

TOP 10 The Adoration of the Mystic Lamb

St Bavo's cathedral in Ghent is home to one of the greatest cultural treasures of northern Europe. This huge, exquisitely painted polyptych is the masterpiece of the brothers Hubrecht and Jan van Eyck. Its survival is something of a miracle. It was rescued from Protestant vandals in 1566, and from fire in 1822. Parts were carried off by French soldiers in 1794, sold in 1816, then stolen in 1934. Currently undergoing a five-year restoration, the polyptych is still on show, but the occasional panel may be missing.

Sint-Baafskathedraal (Cathedral of St Bavo)

There are several friendly cafés immediately outside the cathedral. More spectacular, though, is the De Foyer café-restaurant on the first floor of the Schouwburg (theatre), with a terrace overlooking the square ***(see p99).***

It is advisable to get there well before closing time: the Villa Chapel shuts promptly. Last tickets are issued 30 minutes before closing, including audioguides (which last 50 minutes).

- *Sint-Baafskathedraal, Sint-Baafsplein*
- *Map Q2*
- *09 269 20 45*
- *Open Apr–Oct: 9:30am–5pm Mon–Sat, 1–5pm Sun; Nov–Mar: 10:30am–4pm Mon–Sat, 1–4pm Sun*
- *Admission: €4, (7–12 yrs €1.50)*

Top 10 Features

1. The Polyptych
2. The Mystic Lamb of God
3. God the Almighty
4. Flowers
5. Mary
6. The Angel-musicians
7. Eve
8. The Idealized City
9. The Inscription
10. The External Panels

1 The Polyptych

The painting consists of 12 panels, four in the centre and four on each of the folding wings. The lower tier depicts the spirituality of the world, and God's chosen people; the upper tier shows the heavenly realm with Adam and Eve on either end.

2 The Mystic Lamb of God

The focus of this panel *(above)* is the Lamb of God, spurting blood on an altar. Four sets of figures approach: virgin martyrs; figures from the New Testament and the Church; patriarchs and prophets of the Old Testament; and confessors of the Faith.

3 God the Almighty

The central figure of the upper tier is God, depicted in a brilliant red robe and a bejewelled mitre, carrying a sceptre and with a crown at his feet. The benign calm and poise of the face radiate throughout the polyptych.

The audioguide to the polyptych (available in several languages) is included in the ticket price. It is long, but extremely informative.

4 Flowers
The numerous flowers make a philosophical point: everything in nature is an expression of God's work. The painter's job was to record it faithfully.

5 Mary
The figure of Mary tells us much about the concept of feminine beauty in medieval times. Fine-featured, absorbed in her reading, she is decked with jewels.

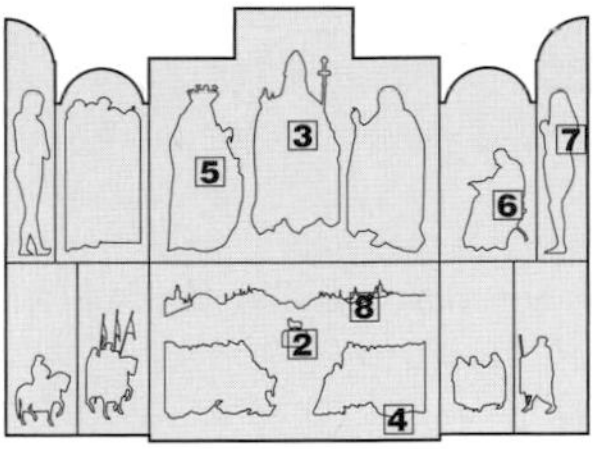

Plan of the polyptych

10 The External Panels
The wings of the painting can be closed. The external panels are tonally quite flat, intensifying the moment they are opened to reveal the sumptuous interior.

6 The Angel-musicians
A heavenly choir sings on one side of the upper tier *(right)*, while on the other, an orchestra of angels plays. The figures are tightly crowded, but the perspective is good.

7 Eve
Jan van Eyck's contemporaries were startled by the realism of his Adam and Eve. Even today, their nudity among the luxuriously clothed figures is striking. Beautifully lit from the right, they show the painter's profound understanding of the human form.

8 The Idealized City
To the rear of the central panel rise the towers and spires of the heavenly city, Jerusalem.

9 The Inscription
In the 19th century, a verse inscription by the two brothers, thought to be original, was uncovered on the frame.

Influence on European Art
Flemish painters, Jan van Eyck in particular, are sometimes credited with inventing oil painting. This is an exaggeration, but certainly they perfected the technique. Antonello da Messina, the Italian credited with pioneering oil painting in Italy, is believed to have learnt his skills from Flemish artists. As a result of these contacts, the advantages of oil painting over tempera or fresco became clear. Italian artists adopted oil painting, and Italian art accelerated toward the High Renaissance.

For more on St Bavo's cathedral **See p95**

Antwerp Cathedral

Antwerp Cathedral is the largest Gothic church in the Low Countries – also one of the most beautiful. Its dainty wedding-cake spire, rising up from a medieval market square, is still a major landmark in the city. The cathedral took 170 years to build, and even then was not complete. It was the church of the wealthy guilds, richly adorned with their shrines, reliquaries and altarpieces. Gutted by fire and vandals in the 16th and 18th centuries, the cathedral still has a number of major treasures, chief among them two magnificent triptychs by Rubens.

The West Door

There are plenty of cafés, bars and restaurants in the streets surrounding the cathedral. One tavern, Het Vermoeide Model in Lijnwaadmarkt *(see p108)*, is actually built up against the cathedral walls. Het Kathedraalcafé in Torfbrug has a pleasant terrace and an interior decorated with statues of saints and other religious paraphernalia *(see p109)*.

Listen out for the carillon bells – the set of 49 bells that play tunes on the hour. In the summer, regular carillon concerts are given, when the bells are played from a keyboard.

- *Handschoenmarkt*
- *Map T2*
- *03 213 99 51*
- *Open 10am–5pm Mon–Fri, 10am–3pm Sat, 1–4pm Sun and public hols*
- *Admission: €5, students and over 60s €3, children under 12 free*

Top 10 Features

1. The Spire
2. The Nave
3. The Raising of the Cross
4. The Pulpit
5. Original Murals
6. The Virgin Exalted through Art
7. The Burgundian Window
8. The Cupola
9. The Madonna of Antwerp
10. The Schyven Organ

1 The Spire

The cathedral's dainty and unusual spire was built over about 100 years from the mid 1400s onward. As it rises to its pinnacle at 123 m (404 feet), it shows increasingly daring Gothic style. The only other comparable spire is that of the Hôtel de Ville in Brussels, of a similar date.

2 The Nave

The interior is bright, light and uplifting, largely by virtue of its scale, the expanse of glass, and the simple, soaring space that rises to the rib vaults. Unusually, the columns of the aisle have no capitals, so bend seamlessly to form Gothic arches, creating a serene effect.

3 The Raising of the Cross

This triptych, and the equally impressive *Descent from the Cross* on the other side of the nave, secured Rubens' reputation in Antwerp. The central and right-hand panels display the dynamic energy that was Rubens' hallmark. The left-hand panel shows the grief of Christ's companions.

For more on Rubens **See pp30–31**

4 The Pulpit

Elaborately carved oak pulpits are a feature of many Belgian churches. The subject of this one, the propagation of the faith in the "four" continents, is tackled with extraordinary ambition – a riot of birds, trees, textile swags, angels, saints and symbolic figures.

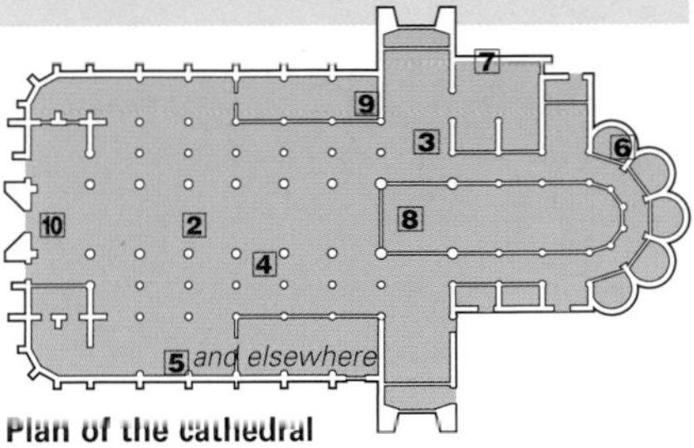

Plan of the cathedral

5 Original Murals

The cathedral was once bright with murals, but over time they fell away or were overpainted. Restoration has revealed patches of the originals.

6 The Virgin Exalted through Art

In the late 19th century, the cathedral was rescued from neglect by massive restoration. In some cases this was overzealous, but the effort to recreate a medieval effect in some of the chapels behind the choir is admirable. Albert de Vriendt's fine triptych shows the "Eyckian" revival at its best.

7 The Burgundian Window

A fair amount of the cathedral's original stained glass has survived. This is the oldest window, dating from 1503 *(below)*. It depicts Philip the Handsome and Joanna of Castile, with their patron saints behind them.

8 The Cupola

From outside, the dome looks like a tiered black onion. Inside *(left)*, its logic is clear: the glass tiers let in light to illuminate the *Assumption of the Virgin* (1647), Cornelis Schut's impressive ceiling painting. The effect is of looking straight up into the heavens.

9 The Madonna of Antwerp

This exceptional little wooden statue has been a focus of devotion since the 16th century, and has a changing wardrobe of robes and crowns.

10 The Schyven Organ

This impressive instrument is housed in a magnificent 17th-century case created by three leading sculptors of the day.

Iconoclasts and French Revolutionaries

Antwerp Cathedral was once richly decorated; two episodes have rendered it rather more austere. The first, in the 1560s, was the onslaught of Protestant zealots, or "iconoclasts", who set about ridding churches of statues, paintings and relics. The second wave occurred in the 1790s, when the forces of the French Revolution went about demolishing churches, or putting them to secular use as stables, warehouses, barracks, law courts, and factories.

TOP 10 Rubenshuis, Antwerp

In 1610, Peter Paul Rubens (1577–1640) – court painter, recently returned from Italy, and newly married – found himself in a position to buy a large house, where he lived and worked until his death. After centuries of neglect, the house was rescued by the City of Antwerp in 1937, and has since been refurbished and refurnished to look as it might have done in Rubens' day. Quite apart from the sheer charm of the place, it provides a rare opportunity to see the physical context in which great works of art were made.

The gardens of the Rubenshuis

Next to the Rubenshuis is an elegant café-restaurant called Rubens Inn, serving snacks as well a substantial lunch menu. For a touch of modern style, the upbeat Grand Café Horta is just around the corner at Hopland 2 *(see p108)*.

The museum gets very busy at peak times, especially in summer. For some chance of a quieter visit, arrive at opening time – although you may find scores of other people have had the same idea.

- *Wapper 9–11*
- *Map U2*
- *03 201 15 55*
- *www.rubenshuis.be*
- *Open 10am–5pm Tue–Sun. Closed Mon and public hols.*
- *Admission: €8 (includes audioguide; ID needed as security); children under 12 free. Free on last Wed of every month*

Top 10 Features

1. The Building
2. The Baroque Portico
3. The Parlour Room
4. The Kitchen
5. The Art Gallery
6. The Dining Room
7. The Large Bedroom
8. The Semi-circular Museum
9. The Little Bedroom
10. Rubens' Studio

1 The Building

The house is in two parts set around an inner courtyard. As you enter, the older, Flemish-style half is to the left – a series of rooms providing the domestic quarters, where Rubens lived and entertained. To the right is the working part of the house, containing Rubens' studio and designed by the artist in grander Baroque style.

2 The Baroque Portico

The massive ornamental screen *(right)* was designed by Rubens in Italianate Baroque style to link the two parts of the house. It also provides a theatrical entrance to the formal garden beyond.

3 The Parlour Room

This room is notable for its wall hangings. Embossed Spanish leather was used as a kind of wallpaper in the houses of the well-to-do.

4 The Kitchen

This charming little kitchen, with its tiled walls and open fireplace, is typical of Flanders. Note the pothooks with ratchets, designed to adjust the height of cooking vessels over the fire. The robust traditions of Flemish cuisine were forged in such kitchens.

7 The Large Bedroom

This is the room in which Rubens died. The beautiful oak-and-ebony curio cabinet located here is decorated with mythological scenes based on Rubens' work.

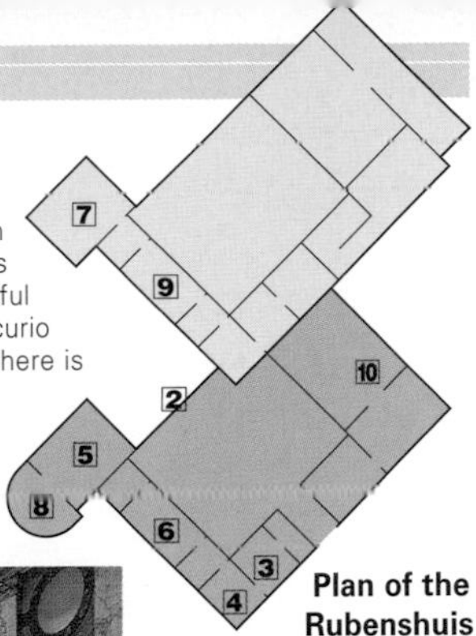

Plan of the Rubenshuis

Key

- Ground floor
- First floor

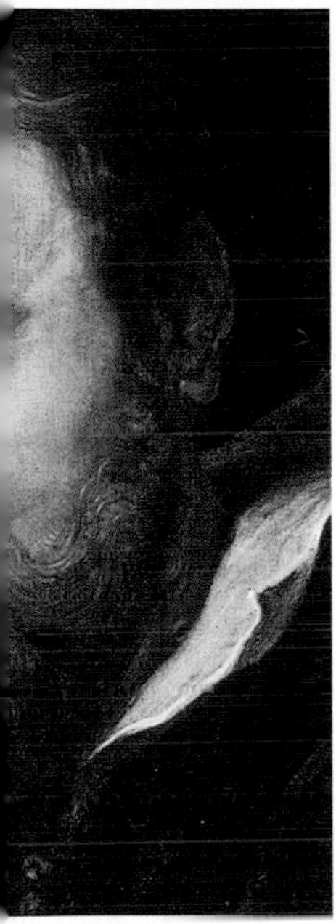

8 The Semi-circular Museum

This elegant marble-lined room *(above)* inspired by the Pantheon in Rome was used by Rubens to exhibit his collection of sculpture. Among the pieces shown today is an antique marble bust of Seneca.

10 Rubens' Studio

In this large and impressive room *(above)*, Rubens worked with a team of assistants and apprentices to maintain his huge productivity. Pictures shown here include the exhilarating but unfinished *Henry IV in the Battle of Ivry* (c.1628–30).

5 The Art Gallery

A painting exhibited here, *The Art Gallery of Cornelis van der Geest*, shows how Rubens' own gallery might have looked – every inch of wall space hung with pictures.

9 The Little Bedroom

The most eye-catching item in this room is the 17th-century box bed *(above)* in which people slept half sitting-up to promote good digestion.

6 The Dining Room

Eating and drinking played a central role in the social habits of Rubens' day *(right)*. A highlight here is a self-portrait of the artist *(main image)*, one of just four in existence.

Swagger and Verve

Rubens began training as an artist aged 13, but it was an eight-year stay in Italy that transformed him. His work chimed with the grandeur and swagger of Baroque architecture and the Counter-Reformation, also with the luxurious lifestyle of the European aristocracy. Working with ceaseless energy, he and his assistants produced over 2,000 major paintings in his lifetime.

The best collections of Rubens' work are in the fine arts museums of Brussels and Antwerp **See pp34–5**

Left **Sint-Janshospitaal** Right **Musée David et Alice van Buuren**

TOP 10 Art Galleries

1 Musées Royaux des Beaux-Arts, Brussels

Brussels' royal museum of fine art holds rich collections of such artists as Brueghel, Rubens and Jordaens *(below)*. It also exhibits 19th-century masterpieces in the Musée Fin-de-Siècle and many fine Art Nouveau pieces in the outstanding Gillion Crowet Collection *(see pp12–15)*.

***The King Drinks* by Jacques Jordaens**

2 Musée Magritte, Brussels

Housed in the Neo-Classical Altenloh Hotel, this museum is the world's most comprehensive collection of René Magritte's oil paintings, drawings, advertising posters, sculptures, films and photographs. Private collectors often loan works to supplement the main collection *(see p15)*.

3 Musée Constantin Meunier, Brussels

The suburban home of the late-19th-century sculptor Constantin Meunier has been turned into a gallery devoted to his work; it leaves the visitor in no doubt of his gifts and the pungency of his social criticism *(see p79)*.

4 Musée David et Alice van Buuren, Brussels

A private collection of art is presented in its original setting: a charming Art Deco home with a beautiful garden *(see p77)*.

5 Groeningemuseum, Bruges

Bruges' main gallery is celebrated above all for its superb collection of paintings by Flemish Masters of the late medieval "Golden Age". A small, easily digestible museum *(see pp24–5)*.

6 Sint-Janshospitaal, Bruges

A superb collection of paintings by Flemish Primitive Hans Memling was originally commissioned for the chapel of this medieval hospital to bring solace to the sick. The conjoining wards and chapel have been restored, giving these works a fascinating context *(see pp24–5)*.

***Les Troncs Gris* by Léon Spilliaert**

Preceding pages **Guildhouse roofs, Antwerp**

7 Museum voor Schone Kunsten (MSK), Ghent

Ghent's museum of fine arts is a bit of a mixed bag, but has a handful of outstanding pieces; just a stone's throw from SMAK, it forms part of a rewarding double act *(see p97)*.

8 Stedelijk Museum voor Actuele Kunst (SMAK), Ghent

This acclaimed gallery of contemporary art not only mounts cutting-edge temporary exhibitions, but also has a remarkable permanent collection. The works on display are guaranteed to provoke a reaction from aficionados and the unconverted alike *(see p97)*.

Stedelijk Museum voor Actuele Kunst

9 Musée d'Ixelles, Brussels

This small but rewarding collection of art boasts names like Rembrandt, Toulouse-Lautrec and Picasso, as well as leading Belgian artists such as Léon Spilliaert *(left)*. The museum is located in Ixelles, south of the city centre *(see p78)*.

10 Museum van Hedendaagse Kunst (MUHKA), Antwerp

The location of this contemporary art gallery, in the up-and-coming former dockland area in the south of the city, sets the tone for what lies inside. A ground-breaking museum *(see p106)*.

Top 10 Works Outside Galleries

1 The Adoration of the Mystic Lamb (1432)
Jan and Hubrecht van Eyck's masterpiece *(see pp26–7)*.

2 The Raising of the Cross (1609–10)
Wonderful triptych by Pieter Paul Rubens *(see p28)*.

3 The Descent from the Cross (1611–14)
Rubens' heartrending triptych contrasts Christ's death with the Nativity *(see p28)*.

4 Madonna and Child (1504–5)
Michelangelo sculpture of mesmeric dignity *(see p86)*.

5 Baroque Pulpit (1699)
Hendrik Verbruggen's elaborately carved pulpit in Brussels' cathedral *(see p68)*.

6 The History of Bruges (1895)
In the Stadhuis of Bruges *(see pp22–3)*, 12 superb Neo-Medievalist murals by Albert and Julien De Vriendt.

7 The Thinker (c.1905)
A copy of Rodin's statue on a tomb in Laeken Cemetery, Brussels. *Parvis Notre-Dame, 1020 BRU (Laeken) • Map F1 • Open 8:30am–4:30pm daily*

8 Hergé Mural (1983)
A cartoon mural decorating Stockel metro station is one of Hergé's last works before his death. *Stockel Metro, Brussels • Map G2*

9 Fountain of Kneeling Youths (1898)
Georges Minne's best-known work. *Emile Braunplein (in front of the Belfort, Ghent)*

10 Nos Vieux Trams Bruxellois (1978)
Paul Delvaux's contribution to putting art in the metro. *Bourse Station, Brussels*

For more on the Belgian Symbolists **See p15**

Left ***The Assumption*** **by Rubens** Right ***Adoration of the Mystic Lamb*** **by the van Eyck brothers**

TOP 10 Belgian Artists

1 Jan van Eyck

The sheer technical brilliance and almost photographic detail of work by Jan van Eyck (c.1390–1441) are self-evident in paintings such as *Madonna with Canon Joris van der Paele* *(see p25)* and *The Adoration of the Mystic Lamb* *(see pp26–7)*. Van Eyck's work had a major impact on Italian art, and helped fuel the Renaissance.

2 Rogier van der Weyden

One of the leading Flemish "Primitives," Rogier van der Weyden (c.1400–64) is best known for the intense emotion of his work, such as *The Seven Sacraments* in the Koninklijk Museum voor Schone Kunsten, Antwerp *(see p103)*. Working mainly in Brussels, he became the leading painter after the death of van Eyck.

Laurent Froimont **by Rogier van der Weyden**

3 Hans Memling

German-born Hans Memling (c.1433–94) was probably trained by Rogier van der Weyden in Brussels before moving to Bruges, where he spent the rest of his life. Memling went on to become one of the most successful artists of his day *(see pp24–5)*.

4 Pieter Brueghel the Elder

During the 16th century, Flemish artists turned to Italy for inspiration, which muddied their distinctive north European vision. But Pieter Brueghel (c.1525–69) rejected this trend and painted in a personal style based on what he saw around him. His depictions of rural villages have an affectionate charm and honest naivety.

5 Peter Paul Rubens

Almost all the best Flemish artists trained in Italy in the 16th century, and no one made more of this experience than Peter Paul Rubens (1577–1640). He combined his prodigious Flemish technique with Italian flourish to produce art full of verve and dynamism.

6 Antoon van Dyck

A colleague and friend of Rubens, Antoon van Dyck (1599–1641) matched many of Rubens' skills, and addressed a similar range of subject matter. Van Dyck, however, is best known for his portraits. He became court painter to Charles I of England, who rewarded him with a knighthood.

***Pieta* by Antoon van Dyck**

7 Jacob Jordaens

After Rubens' death, another of his collaborators Jacob Jordaens (1593–1678) became Antwerp's leading painter. He is best remembered for allegorical paintings expressing the *joie-de-vivre* of the Baroque age.

8 James Ensor

The work of James Ensor (1860–1949) has earned him a reputation as one of art history's great eccentrics. His paintings incorporate skeletons, masks and hideous caricatures *(see p13)*.

9 Paul Delvaux

Some memorable images of Surrealism came from the studio of Paul Delvaux (1897–1994). He is famous for his sensual, trance-like pictures of somnolent nudes in incongruous settings.

10 René Magritte

The dreamlike paintings of René Magritte (1898–1967) rank alongside Salvador Dali's work as archetypal Surrealism. The Magritte Museum *(see p15)* displays paintings by the artist, plus photographs, drawings and archives.

Top 10 Lesser-known Belgian Artists

1 Constantin Meunier

Sculptor and painter (1831–1905) known for bronzes of factory workers *(see p79)*.

2 Théo van Rysselberghe

Painter (1862–1926) who used Pointillism to develop a polished and distinctive style.

3 Émile Claus

Post-Impressionist painter (1849–1924) famous for rural scenes of sparkling clarity, achieved through a technique that he called "Luminism".

4 Jean Delville

One of the most inventive of the Symbolists (1867–1953), famed for brilliantly coloured visions of Satanic forces.

5 Léon Frédéric

A Symbolist (1856–1940) whose works combine social realism with poetic vision.

6 Fernand Khnopff

A painter (1858–1928) whose enigmatic Symbolist work is suffused with suppressed sexuality.

7 Léon Spilliaert

A Symbolist (1881–1946) of great originality, whose works, often black and white, are instantly recognizable.

8 Rik Wouters

A painter and sculptor (1882–1916) whose work is full of light, verve and charm.

9 Constant Permeke

A painter (1886–1952) of the second phase of the Sint-Martens-Latem school *(see pp14–15)*, his work has a social edge and dark, gritty textures.

10 Panamarenko

True to Surrealist traditions, this artist (born 1940) creates machines, such as space ships, and stages clearly doomed attempts to make them work.

For the best art galleries **See pp34–5**

Left **Musée Charlier** Right **Musée des Instruments de Musique**

TOP 10 Museums

1 Musées Royaux d'Art et d'Histoire, Brussels

Belgium's collection of historic national and international treasures is housed in this palatial building. It includes an impressive array of medieval church treasures (in the Salle aux Trésors), tapestries, Art Nouveau sculpture and jewellery, antique costumes and archaeological finds. One of three museums in the Parc du Cinquantenaire *(see p77)*.

2 Musée des Instruments de Musique, Brussels

Housed in a classic Art Nouveau department store, perched on a ridge overlooking the city, "Le mim" is one of Brussels' must-see sights. More than 1,200 multifarious exhibits are enhanced by listening to their sounds on a personal iPad-like guidance device *(see pp16–17)*.

Musée Royal de l'Armée et d'Histoire Militaire

3 Musée Horta, Brussels

The full artistic potential of Art Nouveau is apparent in this museum – formerly the house and offices of Victor Horta, the father of Art Nouveau architecture *(see pp18–19)*.

4 Musée Charlier, Brussels

A rare opportunity to see inside one of Brussels' *maisons de maître* (mansions). As well as a fine collection of antique furniture, the Hôtel Charlier contains many reminders of its days as a meeting place for the avant-garde set in the early 20th century *(see p68)*.

5 Gruuthusemuseum, Bruges

For over 100 years this historic house has served as a museum presenting an ever-growing collection of artifacts from daily life – both lowly and grand – dating from Bruges' medieval Golden Age to the 19th century. The exhibits have benefited from a remodelling of the museum *(see p86)*.

6 Museum voor Volkskunde, Bruges

See life as it was lived by the ordinary folk of Bruges in the often threadbare 19th and early 20th centuries. Fascinating collections of household items, as well as some complete workshops, bring home the extraordinary changes of the last century and a half *(see p89)*.

The Cinquantenaire

Brabant Raising the National Flag – the symbolic bronze sculpture crowning the central arch of the Palais du Cinquantenaire.

The era of great international fairs was launched by the Great Exhibition in Hyde Park, London, in 1851. King Léopold II decided to mount a similar exhibition to mark the 50th anniversary (cinquantenaire) *of the founding of Belgium in 1880. The site chosen was marshland to the east of the historic centre of Brussels. A pair of exhibition complexes, linked by a monumental semi-circular colonnade, was commissioned from Gédéon Bordiau. The project was not completed in time for the 1880 jubilee, but building continued and the site was used for subsequent fairs. The central triumphal arch – topped by a quadriga reminiscent of Berlin's Brandenburg Gate – was completed in 1905 to mark Belgium's 75th anniversary. Bordiau's barrel-vaulted exhibition hall houses the Musée Royal de l'Armée et d'Histoire Militaire. Its twin to the south was destroyed by fire in 1946; its replacement now forms part of the Musées Royaux d'Art et d'Histoire. The Parc and Palais du Cinquantenaire also contain Autoworld* (see p77)*, as well as two curiosities: the Atelier de Moulage* (see p41) *and the Pavillon Horta* (see p45).

7 Design Museum Gent, Ghent

Anyone interested in antique furniture and the history of the decorative arts will love this delightful museum, which follows changing styles from the domestic elegance of the 17th century to the jocular irreverence of Milanese Post-Modernism *(see p96)*.

8 Huis van Alijn, Ghent

This evocative folk museum, set out in almshouses founded by the Alijn family in the 14th century, has become a major repository for a huge range of artifacts that were part and parcel of the lives of ordinary Flanders people in past centuries *(see p96)*.

9 Museum Plantin-Moretus, Antwerp

Within a century of Gutenberg's breakthrough in European printing by means of movable type, this 16th-century printing house had become a leader of the publishing revolution. Among the presses and engraving plates, visitors can still detect the possibilities of the spread of knowledge that printing promised *(see p104)*.

10 Museum Aan de Stroom (MAS), Antwerp

This dynamic construction of perspex and red sandstone is packed with ethnographic and folkloric treasures – plus there are great city views from the rooftop *(see p103)*.

Design Museum, Ghent

For unusual museums **See pp40–41**

Left **Koninklijk Museum voor Midden-Afrika** Right **Musée de Tram Bruxellois**

TOP 10 Unusual Museums

1 Centre Belge de la Bande Dessinée, Brussels

As the Belgian Centre of the Comic Strip is the first to admit, comic strips were not invented in Belgium, but the nation has certainly taken them to its heart, and produced a string of gifted artist-writers, the most famous being Hergé, creator of Tintin. The museum is in an Art Nouveau building by Horta *(see pp20–21)*.

2 Musée du Jouet, Brussels

Teddy bears, dolls, miniature farmyards, rocking horses – this toy museum is an Aladdin's cave of delights with exhibits from the 1850s to the present *(see p70)*.

3 Musée Wiertz, Brussels

The studio of the 19th-century painter Antoine Wiertz reveals him as an artist of great self-delusion. Offended by rejection in Paris, he wanted to see Brussels usurp Paris as the capital of Europe. The fact that the European Parliament building is on his doorstep seems spookily visionary *(see p79)*.

4 Musée des Égouts, Brussels

Brussels' sewer museum gives an insight into the massive public works that made the city safe to live in during the late 19th century. Visits to a small portion of the vast network by guided tour only. *Pavillon de l'Octroi, Porte d'Anderlecht • Map A3 • 02 500 7031 • Open 10am–5pm Tue–Fri (guided tours Thu & Fri) • Adm charge*

5 Musée du Tram Bruxellois, Brussels

With dozens of trams, ancient and modern, lining the silent platforms of an old tram depot, a visit to this museum is a bit like wandering into one of Delvaux's Surrealist paintings. It has far more appeal than its subject matter may suggest *(see p78)*.

6 ModeMuseum (MoMu), Antwerp

"You are what you wear" is the philosophy behind this museum in Antwerp's fashion district. The collection presents the theory and practice of fashion, from 16th-century lacemaking to today's cutting-edge Belgian designers, through imaginative displays. *Nationalestraat 28 • Map T2 • 03 470 27 70 • www.momu.be • Open 10am–6pm Tue–Sun • Adm charge*

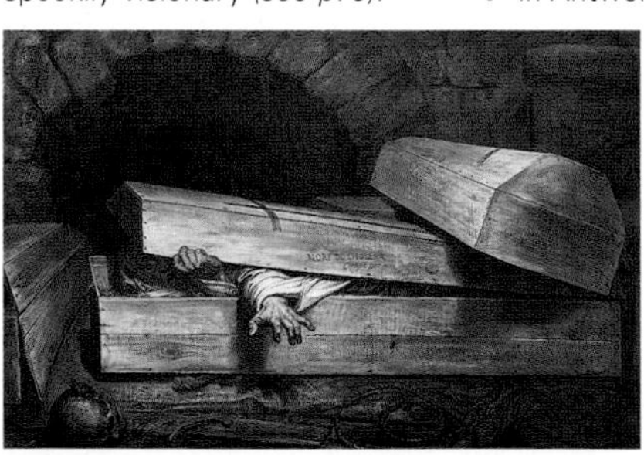

The Overhasty Burial **by Antoine Wiertz**

7 Béguinage d'Anderlecht, Brussels

Many of these pious settlements for single women still survive *(see p86)*. This small one serves as a museum evoking their lives. Unforgettable charm *(see p80)*.

Béguinage d'Anderlecht

8 Koninklijk Museum voor Midden-Afrika (KMMA), Brussels (Tervuren)

The bold scale of this museum in a vast, elegant Neo-Classical palace almost matches Belgium's ambitions as a colonial power in the Congo. A substantial renovation project will keep the museum closed until 2016. ✆ *Leuvensesteenweg 13, 3080 Tervuren • Map H2 • 02 769 52 11 • www.africamuseum.be*

9 Arentshuis, Bruges

This museum owes its existence to the gift to Bruges by the British artist Frank Brangwyn (1867–1956) of a large collection of his own paintings and prints. The result is both unusual and rewarding, as Brangwyn had a highly distinctive eye and was a brilliant draughtsman *(see p87)*.

10 Frietmuseum, Bruges

Learn about the humble potato, from its origins in South America 10,000 years ago to its modern iconic status as Belgium's favourite deep-fried vegetable *(see p80)*.

Top 10 Unusual Museum Collections

1 Musée Boyadjian du Coeur

The heart as symbol – a heart surgeon's collection of artifacts. ✆ *1, 2, 3: Musées Royaux d'Art et d'Histoire, Brussels (see p77)*

2 La Salle aux Trésors

Fabulous medieval treasures, spectacularly lit.

3 Magasin Wolfers

Valuable collection of Art Nouveau artifacts.

4 Atelier de Moulage

Workshop producing plaster-cast copies of classic sculptures. ✆ *Parc du Cinquantenaire, Brussels (see p77)*

5 The Mannekin-Pis Costume Collection

A selection of the 815 costumes created for the little statue. ✆ *Maison du Roi, Brussels (see p8)*

6 Dinosaur Skeletons

The famous Iguanodons of Bernissart. ✆ *Musée des Sciences Naturelles, Brussels (see p80)*

7 Books Censored by the Inquisition

"Heretical" books ruthlessly swathed in black ink. ✆ *Maison d'Erasme, Brussels (see p80)*

8 Ex Voto Offerings

Tiny models of animals and body parts once used to plead for heavenly intercession. ✆ *Béguinage d'Anderlecht (see p80)*

9 Historic Rubbish

Display showing the archaeological value of waste. ✆ *Archeologisch Museum, Bruges. Mariastraat 36a • Map K5 • Open 9:30am–12:30pm, 1:30–5pm Tue–Sun • Adm charge*

10 Identity Tags for Abandoned Babies

Tragic mementos of mothers and children. ✆ *Maagdenhuis, Antwerp (see p106)*

Left **Onze-Lieve-Vrouwekathedraal, Antwerp** Right **Église Notre-Dame du Sablon, Brussels**

TOP 10 Churches

1 Cathédrale des Saints Michel et Gudule, Brussels

Brussels' honey-coloured Gothic cathedral is a sanctuary of calm after the bustle of the Grand Place. Used for royal weddings and funerals *(see p68)*.

2 Église Saint-Jacques-sur-Coudenberg, Brussels

One of Brussels' most distinctive churches occupies a prominent position overlooking the Place Royale: its bell-tower apart, it looks more like a Roman temple than a Christian church *(see p68)*.

3 Église Notre-Dame du Sablon, Brussels

The 15th-century church of the Guild of Crossbowmen is a beautiful example of Brabantine Gothic style, lit by large expanses of stained glass *(see p69)*.

Église Saint-Jean-Baptiste-au-Béguinage

4 Église Saint-Jean-Baptiste au Béguinage, Brussels

The exuberant Flemish Baroque façade of this church contrasts with its history as the focal point of a *béguine* community of women. Something of their charity and moderation still pervades the interior *(see p69)*.

5 Onze-Lieve-Vrouwekerk, Bruges

Bruges' most striking church, with a rocket-like spire in the austere style of Scheldt Gothic. The interior has been tinkered with ceaselessly since the 13th century. Its outstanding treasure is Michelangelo's *Madonna and Child*, donated by a wealthy merchant in 1514 *(see p86)*.

6 Sint-Salvatorskathedraal, Bruges

Both grand and sombre, the tone of this church befits its status as Bruges' cathedral. Although mainly Gothic, Saint Saviour's may date back in origin to early Christian times. The turreted tower was built in Neo-Medieval style in the late 19th century *(see p88)*.

7 Sint-Baafskathedraal, Ghent

Its soaring Gothic interior and Baroque choir give Ghent's impressive cathedral a forceful quality *(see p95)*. It is upstaged, however, by its greatest treasure: Jan and Hubrecht van Eyck's magnificent *Adoration of the Mystic Lamb (see pp26–7)*.

At most churches, admission charges apply only to their museums or special exhibits.

Sint-Niklaaskerk

8 Sint-Niklaaskerk, Ghent

The interior of Ghent's most attractive and imposing church has been scrubbed clean by a programme of restoration, resulting in a light and joyous space that makes the most of the robust Gothic stonework *(see p95)*.

9 Onze-Lieve-Vrouwekathedraal, Antwerp

With only one of its two towers finished, Antwerp's cathedral bears the battle scars of its centuries-long struggle for completion, but the immense interior gives a clear indication of the scale of its creators' ambitions. It also provides an apt setting for two stunning triptychs by Rubens, as well as some ravishing late-19th-century paintings *(see pp28–9)*.

10 Sint-Jacobskerk, Antwerp

The richly ornate interior of this church bears testimony to the fact that it was frequented by the well-to-do during Antwerp's 17th-century heyday – among them, Rubens, who was buried in his family chapel here *(see pp104–5)*.

Top 10 Architectural Styles

1 Romanesque
10th–12th centuries. Semi-circular arches and hefty columns. The style is called "Norman" in Britain.

2 Gothic
13th–16th centuries. Pointed arches allowed for lighter structures.

3 Scheldt (or Scaldian) Gothic
13th–14th centuries. An early, rather austere version of Gothic typical of northern Belgium (around the River Scheldt).

4 Brabantine and Flamboyant Gothic
14th–15th centuries. A daintier form of Gothic, used for town halls like Bruges' Stadhuis.

5 Renaissance
15th–17th centuries. An elegant style taking its inspiration from Greek and Roman architecture.

6 Baroque
17th–18th centuries. A lavish interpretation of Classical style, full of exuberance and swagger.

7 Neo-Classical
18th–19th centuries. Classical revisited again, even more determined to emulate Greek and Roman temples.

8 Neo-Gothic
19th-century. Gothic style revisited. Adopted particularly by the Catholic Revival.

9 Art Nouveau
Late 19th–early 20th centuries. A florid, organic style, an effort to create an utterly new approach: hence "new art".

10 Art Deco
1920s–1930s. A brash, angular but glamorous style. Name is based on a decorative arts exhibition in Paris in 1925.

Left **Musée Horta, detail of the ironwork bannisters** Right **Musée des Instruments de Musique**

TOP 10 Art Nouveau Buildings in Brussels

1 Musée Horta

The home and studio of the great maestro of Art Nouveau architecture, Victor Horta, serves as a master-class in the form *(see pp18–19)*.

2 Hôtel Tassel

Designed by Victor Horta in 1893–5, this is considered the first Art Nouveau house. Up to this point, the well-to-do who commissioned new private mansions in the mushrooming Belgian suburbs adopted any style going: Moorish, Medieval, Tuscan, whatever. Horta extrapolated from this "eclectic" style to evolve something more integrated and considered. The private mansion of a bachelor engineer, Hôtel Tassel was carefully tailored to all aspects of his lifestyle, but this individualized approach also made it less adaptable for subsequent owners. *Rue Paul-Émile Janson 6, 1050 BRU (Ixelles)*

3 Maison de Paul Cauchie

Behind a façade combining geometric shapes with dreamy Art Nouveau murals lies the home of little-known painter Paul Cauchie (1875–1952). *Rue des Francs 5, 1040 BRU (Etterbeek) • 02 733 86 84 • Open 1st weekend of every month, 10am–1pm, 2–5:30pm; May–Aug: 6–9pm Tue • Adm charge*

Hôtel Hannon

4 Hôtel Saint-Cyr

Art Nouveau tended toward excess, and this accusation might certainly be levelled at this house – all loops and curves, with a circular picture window on the top floor. It was designed for painter Saint-Cyr in 1900. *Square Ambiorix 11, 1000 BRU (Brussels)*

5 Hôtel Hannon

Swathes of Art Nouveau mansions were cleared from Brussels when the style fell from favour. Hôtel Hannon, built in 1902, is a rarity because some of the internal decorations have survived – and also because the public can gain access to the interior. *Ave de la Jonction 1, 1060 BRU (Saint-Gilles) • Map G2 • 02 538 42 20 • Open 11am–6pm Wed–Fri, 1–6pm Sat & Sun • Adm charge*

6 Hôtel Ciamberlani

The artist Albert Ciamberlani (1864–1956) was one of those responsible for the huge mural in the triumphal colonnade of the Cinquantenaire building *(see p39)*. He employed Paul Hankar (1859–1901), a key Art Nouveau architect, to build his house and studio in 1897. The façade combines iron, stone and brick for a highly individual decorative effect. *Rue Defacqz 48, 1050 BRU (Ixelles)*

Note that Hôtel Tassel, Hôtel Saint-Cyr and Hôtel Ciamberlani are private residences, and are not open to the public.

7 Musée des Instruments de Musique, Brussels

Art Nouveau was also called "Style Liberty", after the famous London store. Brussels' "Old England" store was named to echo this vogue. The building houses the Museum of Musical Instruments *(see pp16–17)*.

8 Centre Belge de la Bande Dessinée

Victor Horta designed the Magasins Waucquez, a textile shop, in 1903. Rescued in the 1970s, it has found new life as the famous comic-strip museum *(see pp20–21)*.

Centre Belge de la Bande Dessinée

9 Le Falstaff

This famous restaurant and drinking palace opposite the Bourse dates from 1903, and still powerfully evokes the era in which it was created. The interior is rich in Art Nouveau detail, seen in the stained glass, mirrors, lamp fittings and furniture *(see p72)*.

10 Hôtel Solvay

The 33-year-old Victor Horta was still fairly unknown when he was commissioned to design this house by the industrialist Ernest Solvay. Its free-flowing form, with swirling wrought iron and a remarkably fluid use of stonework, established Horta as a master of the Art Nouveau style.

Avenue Louise 224, 1050 BRU (Ixelles)

Top 10 Architectural Wonders

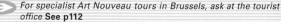

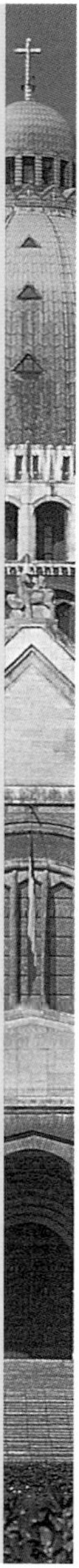

1 Jeruzalemkerk, Bruges
A Byzantine-influenced church inspired by a pilgrimage to the Holy Land *(see p89)*.

2 Palais de Justice, Brussels
Joseph Poelaert threw every Neo-Classical style in the book at this vast and domineering monument to justice *(see p70)*.

3 Pavillon Chinois, Tour Japonaise, Brussels
Two beautiful oriental buildings rise up incongruously from the Parc de Laeken *(see p77)*.

4 Serres Royales, Brussels
Architecturally magnificent royal greenhouses built in the 1870s *(see p80)*.

5 Cinquantenaire Arch
A staggering 45-m (147-ft) high Neo-Classical arch with a huge quadriga on top *(see p39)*.

6 Hôtel Saint-Cyr, Brussels
Brussels' weirdest Art Nouveau building *(see opposite)*.

7 Centraal Station, Antwerp
Louis Delacenserie's station is a delicious pot-pourri of Neo-Classical styles *(see p106)*.

8 MAS, Antwerp
Designed by Dutch architects Willem Jan Neutelings and Michiel Riedijk, this striking building resembles giant, red Lego bricks *(see p103)*.

9 The Atomium, Brussels
A giant model of a crystal of iron, created for the 1958 Universal Exposition *(see p77)*.

10 Basilique Nationale du Sacré-Coeur, Brussels
There is something strangely soulless about this massive 20th-century church *(see p80)*.

For specialist Art Nouveau tours in Brussels, ask at the tourist office **See p112**

Left **Counts Egmont and Hoorn, Place du Petit Sablon, Brussels** Right **The Revolution of 1830**

Top 10 Moments in Belgian History

1 50s BC: Julius Caesar

The Roman army suffered repeated setbacks in its struggle against the courageous "Belgae", but in the end Rome won out, and Belgium flourished under the Pax Romana of provincial rule for 400 years.

2 AD 843: Treaty of Verdun

After the Romans came the Franks, whose empire reached its apogee under Charlemagne. After his death, his homeland was split by treaty along the River Scheldt – the division from which Flanders and Wallonia would evolve.

3 1302: Battle of the Golden Spurs

France dominated Flanders for much of the medieval period, eventually resulting in popular revolt. At the Battle of the Golden Spurs, a Flemish rebel force humiliated the cream of the French army.

Philip the Good after Rogier van der Weyden

4 1384: Burgundy takes over

When Louis de Male, Count of Flanders, died in 1384, his title was inherited by his son-in-law Philip the Bold (1342–1404), Duke of Burgundy. The powerful dukes of Burgundy gradually extended their control over the Low Countries. Burgundian rule reached a Golden Age under Philip the Good (reigned 1419–67). Bruges, his capital, was the centre of a rich trading empire.

5 1568: Religious strife

Charles V, Holy Roman Emperor and King of Spain, inherited the Burgundian territories, but faced violent opposition there as Protestantism gathered pace. A decisive moment came in 1568, during the reign of Philip II, when Counts Egmont and Hoorn were executed in the Grand Place for opposing the persecution of Protestants. Eventually the territory was divided into Protestant north (the Netherlands) and Catholic south (now Belgium).

6 1815: Battle of Waterloo

When the Spanish Netherlands passed to Austria in 1713, conservative groups began to agitate for Belgian independence. Their revolt was swept aside in 1794 when the French revolutionary armies invaded. The Belgians were divided over the merits of Napoleonic rule, and fought on both sides when Napoleon was finally defeated by the Allies at Waterloo *(see p62)*.

7 1830: The Belgian Revolution

After Waterloo, the Congress of Vienna placed Belgium under Dutch rule, a deeply unpopular solution. Anger boiled over in 1830, independence was declared, and the Dutch army was forced out of Brussels.

8 1914–18: World War I

At the outbreak of World War I, the German army swept into neutral Belgium. The Belgians thwarted their advance by flooding the land. The front settled near the medieval town of Ypres *(see p63)*. Over the next four years, half a million people from both sides died there.

The Front Line at Ypres, World War I

9 1940–44: World War II

History was repeated in May 1940, when the German army launched a *Blitzkrieg* against neutral Belgium to outflank the Maginot Line, which blocked their entry into France. Brussels was liberated in September 1944.

10 1957: Treaty of Rome

Having been unwitting victims of two World Wars, the Belgians were enthusiastic supporters of the Treaty of Rome, which laid the foundations for the European Union. Over time, Brussels has effectively become the "Capital of Europe".

Top 10 Historical Figures

1 Baldwin Iron-Arm
Baldwin (d. 878) became the first Count of Flanders, making Bruges his stronghold.

2 Pieter de Coninck and Jan Breydel
De Coninck, a weaver, and Breydel, a butcher, led the Flemish rebellion against the French, launched in 1302.

3 Philip the Bold
Philip the Bold ushered in the Burgundian era in the Netherlands after inheriting control of Brussels and Flanders.

4 Philip the Good
Philip the Good (reigned 1419–67) founded the Order of the Golden Fleece and was a great patron of the arts.

5 Charles V
Born in Ghent, Charles V (1500–58) forged the largest empire in Europe since Roman times. His press is mixed.

6 Isabella and Albert
The dazzling court of the Infanta Isabella (1566–1633) and Archduke Albert (1559–1621) marked calmer times for Spanish Habsburg rule.

7 Charles of Lorraine
Austrian governor general (ruled 1744–80) credited with bringing the Age of Enlightenment to Brussels.

8 King Léopold I
First king of Belgium (ruled 1831–65), popular for his total commitment to the task.

9 King Léopold II
Second king of Belgium (ruled 1865–1909) *(see p78)*.

10 Paul-Henri Spaak
Socialist prime minister during the post-war years, Spaak (1899–1972) played a central role in the creation of the European Community.

For the best exposition of the historical evolution of Brussels, visit the Maison du Roi **See p8**

Left **Hergé** Right **Johnny Hallyday**

Top 10 Famous Belgians

1 Gerard Mercator

Most school maps of the world are still based on the "Mercator projection" – an ingenious way of representing the spherical globe on a flat page. Mercator (1512–94) is also credited with creating the first "atlas", a word he introduced.

2 Georges Simenon

One of the world's best-selling authors, Simenon (1903–89) was born and bred in Liège. His most famous creation, Inspector Maigret, appeared in 75 of his 400 novels.

Queen Astrid

3 Queen Astrid

Prince Léopold of Belgium married the beautiful Swedish princess Astrid in 1926. By the time of their coronation in 1934, they had three young children, but tragedy struck the following year when she was killed in a car accident in Switzerland, aged 29.

4 Hergé

Georges Remi (1907–83) was a self-taught illustrator from the Brussels suburb of Etterbeek. In 1929 he published a story called *Tintin au Pays des Soviets*, and Belgium's most celebrated comic-strip character was born. Since then, 200 million Tintin books have been sold worldwide in some 50 languages. Georges Remi devised his pen name, Hergé, by simply reversing his initials and spelling out the sounds.

5 Jacques Brel

Jacques Brel (1929–78) still ranks in many people's minds as the greatest singer-songwriter in the French language. Although he first made his name in France, he remained loyal to his Belgian origins. The Jacques Brel Foundation in Brussels celebrates his life and work. *Place de la Vieille Halle aux Blés 11 • Map C3 • 02 511 10 20 • www.jacquesbrel.be • Open 10am–6pm Tue–Sat, 11am–6pm Sun. Closed Mon & public holidays • Adm charge*

6 Johnny Hallyday

Although Johnny Hallyday (born 1943) is most famous as the "godfather of French rock 'n' roll", Belgium also claims him: his father was Belgian. In a long career he has sold over 100 million records. He has had a parallel career in film acting, impressing critics with his superb performance in the title role of *L'Homme du Train* (*The Man on the Train*, 2003).

For more on Hergé and Tintin **See pp20–21**

Jacques Brel

7 Eddie Merckx
Cycling is big in Belgium, and no name ranks higher than Eddie Merckx (born 1945), five times winner of the Tour de France (1969–72 and 1974).

8 Jean-Claude Van Damme
A former karate champion, Jean-Claude Van Damme (born 1960) did odd jobs in California, such as delivering pizzas and laying carpets, before making his name with action thrillers like *Cyborg, Kickboxer* (1989) and *Universal Soldier* (1992).

9 Justine Henin-Hardenne
Together with Kim Clijsters *(see below)*, Justine Henin has brought Belgian tennis to a new level. She scored her first Grand Slam victory in the French Open in 2003, going on to win the US Open later the same year – each time in finals against Clijsters.

10 Kim Clijsters
Kim Clijsters' father, Lei, set his daughter on an early road to success when he built her a clay tennis court at their home in Bree, in Limburg province. In 2003, Clijsters became the first Belgian to reach number one in world rankings. She retired in 2012.

Top 10 Slightly Less Famous Belgians

1 Andreas Vesalius
Known as "the father of modern anatomy", Vesalius (1514–64) was physician to Charles V and Philip II of Spain.

2 Adolphe Sax
Best known as inventor of the saxophone, Sax (1814–94) devised a range of innovative musical instruments.

3 Father Damien
A missionary (1840–89) who devoted his life to caring for lepers in Hawaii. He was canonised in 2009 by Pope Benedict XVI.

4 Victor Horta
The innovative Art Nouveau architect credited with bringing the style to maturity *(see pp18–19)*.

5 Léo-Hendrik Baekeland
A chemist (1863–1944) who invented Bakelite, the first totally synthetic plastic.

6 Henri van de Velde
Leading Art Nouveau designer (1863–1957) whose work laid the foundations for the Bauhaus movement.

7 Adrien de Gerlache
Pioneer polar explorer (1866–1934) who led the first expedition to overwinter in Antarctica in 1897–99.

8 Jacky Ickx
One of the great Formula One racing drivers of the 1960s and 1970s (born 1945).

9 Anne Teresa De Keersmaeker
A leading choreographer (born 1960) in the world of contemporary dance.

10 Dries van Noten
A celebrated fashion designer (born 1958) who has helped bring Antwerp to the forefront of *haute couture.*

Left **Ommegang, Brussels** Right **Procession of the Holy Blood, Bruges**

TOP 10 Festivals and Events

1 Ommegang, Brussels

In Brussels' most spectacular parade, some 2,000 participants, dressed as Renaissance nobles, guildsmen, mounted soldiers and entertainers, perform an *ommegang* (tour) in the Grand Place. It's a tradition said to date back to 1549. *First Tue & Thu in July*

Planting of the may tree, Brussels

2 Plantation du Meiboom, Brussels

A jolly slice of ancient folklore dating back to 1213. Led by the Confrérie des Compagnons de Saint-Laurent, dressed in wacky costumes, and accompanied by seven traditional giant figures, the participants parade a may tree around central Brussels, before planting it on the corner of the Rue du Marais and Rue des Sables. *9 Aug (1:30pm onwards)*

3 Foire du Midi, Brussels

This big, rollicking, noisy late-summer fun fair set out along the Boulevard du Midi has the newest rides plus dodgems, roller coasters and all the other old favourites. *Mid-Jul to mid-Aug*

4 Heilig Bloedprocessie, Bruges

Bruges' biggest day out, the Procession of the Holy Blood follows an 800-year-old tradition: 40 days after Easter, the sacred relic of the Holy Blood is paraded around the streets in a colourful, spectacular, but at heart solemn procession featuring sumptuous medieval and biblical costumes. *Ascension Day (May)*

5 Praalstoet van de Gouden Boom, Bruges

First performed in 1958, the Pageant of the Golden Tree takes place in Bruges every five years or so. In a vast costumed parade, the people of the city evoke the glory days of the Burgundian era. *Late Aug (next in 2017)*

6 Reiefeest, Bruges

Bruges' river is the Reie. This festival, held every five years, celebrates its role in the city's history. A series of historical scenes is performed at night at various points beside the water, creating a magical effect and bringing the city's architecture to life. *Last 10 days of Aug (next in 2018)*

7 Gentse Floraliën, Ghent

Every five years, this vast flower show takes place in the Flanders Expo trade fair complex to the south-west of the city centre. Ghent's flower-growing industry is famous above all for its begonias, azaleas, rhododendrons and roses. *Late Apr (next in 2015)*

8 Festival van Vlaanderen
An impressive programme of classical music – as well as jazz, world music and dance – takes place across Flanders every summer and autumn, with performances in the main venues, as well as in churches and other historic buildings. *www.festival.be • Jun–Oct*

9 Toussaint, all Belgium
All Saints' Day is followed by the Jour des Morts, the Day of the Dead – a time when Belgians honour their departed by tidying up the graveyards and filling them with flowers – over 50 million, apparently, mainly chrysanthemums, which glow softly with autumnal colours. *1–2 Nov*

10 Fête de Saint-Nicolas, all Belgium
The Feast of St Nicholas (Sinterklaas in Dutch) is celebrated by children with even greater enthusiasm than Christmas. St Nicholas (the original Santa Claus), dressed as the Bishop of Myra, walks the streets with his blacked-up sidekick Zwarte Piet, and children receive presents, as well as sweets and *speculoos* biscuits. *6 Dec*

Feast of St Nicholas

Top 10 Spectator Sports and Venues

1 Ronde van Vlaanderen
Classic of the cycling calendar. *First Sun in Apr*

2 Liège-Bastogne-Liège
Oldest cycling classic in the World Cup. *Third Sun in Apr*

3 Zesdaagse van Gent
One of the most important meetings for European speed cycling. *'t Kuipke, Citadelpark, Ghent • Map P6 • Late Nov*

4 Ivo Van Damme Memorial Meeting
The most important athletics meeting in the Belgian sports calendar. *Stade Roi Baudouin, Brussels • Map F1 • End Sep*

5 Brussels 20K Race
Brussels' mini-marathon. *Last Sun in May*

6 GDF Suez Diamond Games
Prestigious women's tennis international. *Sportpaleis, Antwerp • Early Dec*

7 Belgian Derby, Ostend
Horsey highlight. *Wellington Renbaan • Middle Sat in Jun*

8 Stade Roi Baudouin
Athletics, cycle meetings and international soccer matches. *Ave du Marathon 135, 1020 BRU (Laeken) • Map F1 • 02 474 39 40*

9 Stade Constant Vanden Stock, Brussels
The home ground of RSC Anderlecht. *Avenue Théo Verbeeck, 1070 BRU (Anderlecht) • Map F2 • 02 529 40 67 (for tickets) • www.rsca.be*

10 Jan Breydel Stadium (Olympiapark), Bruges
Stadium shared by Club Brugge and Cercle Brugge. *Olympialaan 74, 8200 Bruges (Sint-Andries) • 050 40 21 21 • www.clubbrugge.be*

Left **Canal boat trip** Right **Musée du Jouet**

Top 10 Children's Attractions

1 Bruparck, Brussels

Near the Atomium *(see p77)* is an amusement park designed to entertain all the family – with a multi-screen cinema, swimming-pool complex, bars and restaurants, and a "Mini-Europe" of scale models *(see p80)*.

Mini-Europe and the Atomium

2 Centre Belge de la Bande Dessinée, Brussels

Older children will be intrigued by this unusual, somewhat specialist museum; younger children may not be, especially if they speak neither French nor Dutch *(see pp20–21)*.

3 Historic Tram Ride, Brussels

This should appeal to children of all ages. A vintage tram strains and squeaks its way along a 40-km (25-mile) circuit of wooded paths from the Musée du Tram Bruxellois. It operates on Sundays from April to September *(see p79)*.

4 Musée du Jouet, Brussels

Toy museums have a habit of boring children stiff, but this one bucks the trend with its welcoming atmosphere and hands-on exhibits *(see p70)*.

5 Manneken-Pis Costume Collection, Brussels

You may be lucky to find the Mannekin-Pis *(see p10)* on one of his dressed-up days. In any case, it's always fun to see his extraordinary wardrobe in the Maison du Roi *(see p8)*, where about 100 of his 815 outfits are on display.

6 Walibi Belgium

Belgium's premier amusement park, with everything from scary roller coasters and vertical drops to soak-to-the-skin water rides, plus more gentle, traditional tracked car-rides and roundabouts for younger visitors. There is also a multi-pool swimming complex, called Aqualibi, with a host of shoots and tube-runs. *Wavre • Walibi Belgium: 010 42 15 00. Aqualibi: 010 42 16 03 • Opening times vary; see website for details • www.walibi.com • Adm charge*

7 Canal Boat Trips, Bruges and Ghent

From a seat in a canal tour boat, the landmarks of Bruges and Ghent show themselves in a new light. Boats leave from various places in the centre of Bruges *(see p84)* and from the Graslei and Korenlei in Ghent *(see p95)*.

8 Belfort, Bruges
A kind of medieval theme-park experience: the physical challenge of a slightly scary spiral staircase, magnificent views from the top, and the therapeutic shock of colossal noise if the bells ring while you are up there. There may even be a queue to get in *(see p85)*.

9 Sound Factory, Bruges
The various installations at this interactive museum allow kids to create their own pop songs, or even their first symphony, via interactive sound machines and more traditional instruments. The museum's location, on the fifth floor of Bruges' Concertgebouw *(see p61)* also offers great views of the city's skyline. ⊗ *Concertgebouw, 't Zand 34 • Map K5 • 070 22 33 02 • www.sound-factory.be • Open 9:30am–5pm Tue–Sun • Adm charge*

10 Antwerp Zoo
One of the oldest zoos in the world (1843). Special attractions include a sea lion show, elephant bathing, a hippo pond and a hands-on reptile experience. The zoo is also a Centre for Research and Conservation. ⊗ *Koningin Astrid plein 26 • Map V2 • 03 202 45 40 • www.zooantwerpen.be • Open 10am–late afternoon daily (closing times vary seasonally between 4:45 & 7pm) • Adm charge*

Penguins in Antwerp Zoo

Top 10 Other Sights for Children

1 Parc du Cinquantenaire, Brussels
The three major museums in this park have enough variety to appeal to all ages *(see p77)*.

2 mim, Brussels
Music in the headphones changes as you go around – a winning formula *(see pp16–17)*.

3 Scientastic, Brussels
Fascinating exhibition explains principles of science. ⊗ *Bourse Metro Station (level -1) • Map B3 • 02 732 13 36*

4 Musée de Sciences Naturelles, Brussels
Good for the budding scientist, ecologist and dinosaur fanatic *(see p80)*.

5 Musée des Égouts, Brussels
Underground sewer visits – perennially appealing *(see p40)*.

6 Musée du Cacao et du Chocolat, Brussels
See, and taste, chocolate in the making *(see p8)*.

7 Musée des Enfants, Brussels
Popular museum for children aged 4–12. Limited numbers. ⊗ *Rue du Bourgmestre 15, 1050 BRU (Ixelles) • 02 640 01 07*

8 Het Huis van Alijn, Ghent
Magical folk museum *(see p96)*.

9 Het Gravensteen, Ghent
Heavily restored medieval castle, complete with dungeon. ⊗ *Sint-Veerleplein • Map P1 • 09 225 93 06*

10 Aquatopia, Antwerp
Lively aquarium opposite Centraal station. ⊗ *Koningin Astridplein 7 • Map V2 • 03 205 07 50 • www.aquatopia.be • 10am–6pm daily • Adm charge*

Left **Seletion of bottled beers** Right **Belgian chocolates**

TOP 10 Things to Buy

1 Chocolate
Belgian chocolate is justly famous. The manufacturers use high-quality cocoa beans and reintroduce a generous proportion of cocoa butter. They also invented the means to manufacture filled chocolates (or pralines) on an industrial scale. As a result, these superb chocolates are remarkably good value.

Lace-making

2 Lace
There were tens of thousands of lace-makers in 19th-century Belgium, many of them living in penury. That industry was undermined by the invention of lace-making machines, and to some degree it still is. If you want to buy proper, hand-made Belgian lace, go to a reputable shop, insist on a label of authenticity, and expect to pay a high price.

3 Beer
In 1900 there were over 3,200 breweries in Belgium; now there are just over 100, but they still generate an astonishing variety of beers *(see pp58–9)*. The most famous are produced by the Trappist monasteries, but even the lighter, lager-style beers such as Stella Artois and Jupiler are made to a high standard.

4 Biscuits and Pâtisserie
It is hard not to drool in front of the ravishing shop windows of Belgian pâtisseries – and the mouth-watering offerings taste as good as they look. An alternative is to buy some of the equally famed biscuits (cookies) – from a specialist like Dandoy *(see p11)*.

5 Tapestry
Tapestry was one of the great medieval industries of Brussels and Bruges. It is still made on a craft basis, but of course large pieces come at luxury prices.

6 Haute Couture
Over the last two decades, Belgium – Antwerp in particular – has shot to the forefront of the fashion world, with designers such as Ann Demeulemeester, Dries van Noten, Raf Simons and Walter Van Bierendonck. Many of the major designers have their own shops in Antwerp *(see p107)*, but there are plenty of outlets elsewhere, notably in the Rue Dansaert in Brussels *(see p71)*.

7 Children's Clothes

There are numerous shops devoted to children's clothes in Belgium, and their products are irresistible – from hard-wearing romp-around cottons to beautifully made winter jackets and hats, and fun shoes.

8 Diamonds

Over three-quarters of the world's uncut diamonds flow through the exchanges of Antwerp; many of these are cut, polished and mounted there. You could find some bargains – but of course, you have to know what you're doing. If in doubt, consult the Hoge Raad voor Diamant (HRD), which oversees a reliable system of certification. *HRD: www.hrd.be*

9 Antiques and Bric-à-brac

For lovers of everything from old comics and Art Nouveau door handles to exquisite Louis XVI desks and ormolu clocks, Belgium is a happy hunting ground. In Brussels, the full range is on view between the Place du Jeu de Balle and the Place du Grand Sablon *(see p71)*.

10 Tintin Merchandise

Tintin fans can pick up not only the books, but also T-shirts, figurines, games, postcards, mobile phone covers, key rings, stationery, mugs – you name it. The characters are copyright, so high-quality, legally produced goods come at a fairly steep price. There are Tintin Shops in central Brussels and Antwerp.

Tintin figure

Top 10 Suppliers of Chocolates, Biscuits and Pâtisserie

1 Leonidas
One of the nation's favourite chocolatiers. Less rich and less expensive than its rivals in the top league. *www.leonidas.com*

2 Godiva
Maker of luxury chocs, with branches worldwide. *www.godiva.be*

3 Neuhaus
Credited with inventing the praline and the *ballotin* (box). *www.neuhaus.be*

4 Corné Toison d'Or
Fine chocolates, with a national presence and a shop in the Galeries Royales de St-Hubert in Brussels *(see p10)*.

5 Wittamer
Chocolates, cakes and biscuits to die for *(see p72)*. *www.wittamer.com*

6 Pierre Marcolini
Fabulous chocolates, made entirely from raw ingredients. *www.marcolini.be*

7 Mary
Chocolates of exquisite quality. *www.mary.be*

8 Galler
A mass-market but high-standard manufacturer. Its famous *Langues de Chat* (cat's tongues) are shaped in a jokey cat's face.

9 Biscuiterie Dandoy
Supreme biscuit manufacturer, in a class of its own *(see p11)*.

10 Jules Destrooper
Mass market manufacturer of biscuits since 1886. Its distinctive blue-and-white boxes contain such refined delights as "almond thins". *www.destrooper.be*

For shopping tips **See pp71, 90, 98 & 107**

Left **Moules-marinières** Right **Waffles**

Top 10 Culinary Highlights

1 Frites
Belgian *frites* (fries) are, quite simply, the best in the world. They are deep-fried in good-quality oil not once but twice, so they end up golden brown and *bien croustillantes* (crisp). *Frites* can be a side-dish or – served with a dollop of mayonnaise – a meal in themselves.

***Frites* or *frietjes* (in Dutch) with mayonnaise**

2 Shellfish and Crustaceans
Seafood plays a major role in Belgian cuisine. Mussels-and-chips (*moules-frites*) is virtually the national dish. Oysters (raw) and scallops (cooked) are also popular. A favourite lunchtime entertainment is to pick one's way through a *plateau de fruits de mer* (seafood platter).

3 Fish
The North Sea ports are the base for active fishing fleets, which bring in daily catches of sole, skate, sea bass, cod and hake. To see the sheer variety of the catch, visit the Vismarkt (fish market) in central Bruges. Place Sainte-Catherine in Brussels is a centre for fish restaurants.

4 Steak
It may be a standard dish of any restaurant or bistro, but *steak-frites* (steak and chips/fries) can be excellent – just what you need on a cold night. You will understand why the meat is good when you visit a butcher's shop: standards are high, because Belgian customers are knowledgeable and demanding.

5 Steak Américain
Belgians have enough confidence in their beef to eat it raw – as *Steak Américain*. A *toast cannibale* is a snack form of this.

6 Game
Belgian food pays heed to the seasons. Winter is the time for warming game recipes, such as the classic dish *faisan à la brabançonne*, pheasant cooked with caramelized endives. Rabbit, hare, venison, wild boar, pigeon, duck and guinea fowl are also much cherished. Much of the "game" is now farm-raised.

Chicons au gratin (Belgian endive)

7 Cooking with Beer

Several of Belgium's classic dishes are cooked with beer – notably the beef stews called *carbonnades flamandes* or *vlaamse stoverij*. In some restaurants (such as Den Dyver in Bruges, *see p92*), almost the entire menu involves beer.

8 Belgian Endive

A great Belgian invention. When trying to overwinter *chicorée* lettuce in around 1840, a Brussels gardener found it produced succulent, salad-like shoots. They can be eaten raw, but their sweet, slightly bitter flavour really emerges when they are cooked, either as a vegetable accompaniment or in dishes such as *chicons au gratin*. *Chicon* is the French word, *witloof* the Dutch; in English, it's endive or chicory (but it's confusing, as these terms can also refer to lettuce).

9 Pâtisserie

Every village and community in Belgium has a good pâtisserie; most shopping streets have several. These supreme concoctions of fresh fruit, chocolate, cream, *crème pâtissière* and, of course, pastry, are an integral part of Belgian life.

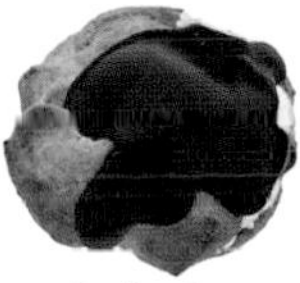

Profiterole

10 Waffles

Waffles (*gaufres/wafels*) are a great Belgian tradition. There are two kinds: the crispy Brussels dusted with icing sugar, or the doughy Liège with sugar crystals baked in. The perfect portable snack, waffles are eaten as a snack at fun fairs, at the seaside and in shopping streets.

Top 10 Classic Belgian Dishes

1 Carbonnades Flamandes/Vlaamse Stoverij
A beef stew cooked in Belgian beer – rich, succulent and sweet, and best eaten with *frites* and mayonnaise.

2 Moules-marinière
Mussels steamed, until they open, in white wine flavoured with celery, onion and parsley; usually served in something resembling a bucket, accompanied by a plate of *frites*.

3 Waterzooi
A creamy, comforting dish of chicken (or fish) with vegetables in broth; a traditional dish of Ghent.

4 Chicons au Gratin
Belgian endives wrapped in ham and baked in a creamy cheese sauce.

5 Anguilles au Vert/ Paling in 't Groen
Eels cooked in a sauce of fresh green herbs.

6 Garnaalkroketten
Deep-fried potato croquettes filled with fresh shrimps; an excellent starter or snack.

7 Salade Liégeoise
A warm salad of potatoes and green beans, or *salade frisée*, with fried bacon bits.

8 Stoemp
Mashed potato mixed with a vegetable, such as carrots or celeriac, or a meat purée.

9 Flamiche aux Poireaux
A quiche-like tart, made with leeks.

10 Jets d'Houblon
Hop-shoots – a spring-time by-product of brewing, usually served in a cream sauce. They taste a bit like asparagus.

Left **Brugs Witbier bottles** Right **Specialist beer shop**

Top 10 Types of Belgian Beer

1 Trappist Beer

In the past, some of Belgium's finest beers were made by the Trappists, a silent order of Cistercian monks. Now it's produced commercially by five breweries with close ties to the monasteries (Chimay, Westmalle, Orval, Rochefort and Westvleteren). Yeast is added at bottling to induce a second fermentation, so pour off carefully in one go to avoid disturbing the sediment.

Chimay

2 Abbey Beer

Other abbeys also produced beer, but unlike the Trappist monasteries, many have licensed them to commercial breweries. Leffe, for example, is now closely connected with InBev. That said, many of the abbey beers are excellent. In addition, there are good "abbey-style" beers, such as Ename, Floreffe and St Feuillien.

3 Witbier/Bière Blanche

Most beer is made from barley, but it can also be made from wheat to produce a distinctive "white beer" to which flavourings such as coriander and orange peel may be added. The result is a light, sparkling and refreshing beer, often served cloudy with sediment. Examples: Hoegaarden, Brugs Tarwebier.

4 Lambic

In the valley of the Senne, the river that flows through Brussels, there is a natural airborne yeast called *Brettanomyces*. For centuries, brewers have simply left their warm wheat-beer wort uncovered during the winter months, and allowed air to deliver the yeast into it. The fermenting beer is then left to mature in wooden casks for a year or more. This creates a very distinctive beer, with a slightly winey edge, called *lambic* – the quintessential beer of Brussels.

5 Gueuze

Lambic of various ages can be blended, and then fermented a second time in the bottle. This produces a beer called *gueuze*, fizzy like champagne and matured a further year or two to accentuate the winey qualities of the original product.

6 Kriek

Lambic can be flavoured with cherries (formerly the cherries of the north Brussels orchards of Schaerbeek), added during fermentation to create a highly distinctive drink called *kriek*; with raspberries, to make *framboise*; or with candy sugar, to make *faro*. Of the three, newcomers may find *faro* the easiest to begin with.

Kriek

There are specialist beer bars in all the main cities, serving hundreds of kinds of beer.

7 Double/Triple

Traditionally, breweries graded their beers by strength: apparently single was around 3%, double 6% and treble 9%. Some breweries – notably the Abbeys – still label their beers double *(dubbel)* and triple *(tripel)*. Double is usually a dark and sweetish brew, triple often golden-blond.

Brugse Tripel

8 Lager-style Beers

Lager, or *pils*, is a bottom-fermented beer: the yeast remains at the bottom of the brew (stronger, heavier ales tend to be top-fermented, which seals in more flavour). Although such light beers may be sniffed at by connoisseurs abroad, in Belgium they are brewed to a high standard. Despite its ubiquity, InBev's famous Stella Artois, brewed at Leuven, is a good-quality lager

Duvel

9 Strong Ales

Some breweries pride themselves on the sheer power of their product. Duvel ("Devil"), at 8.5%, is a famous example. Several lay claim to being the strongest beer in Belgium; at 12%, Bush beer is up there, and to be treated with respect.

10 Christmas Beers

Many of the breweries produce Christmas ales for the festive season. These may just be prettily labelled versions of their usual brew, but may also be enriched ales of high strength.

Top 10 Beer Places

1 Cantillon, Brussels
The quaint old Cantillon brewery is the only working brewery still left in Brussels *(see p80)*.

2 A la Mort Subite, Brussels
A famous café-bar in central Brussels, with a *gueuze* named after it *(see p72)*.

3 Chez Moeder Lambic, Brussels
A justly revered beer-shrine in Saint-Gilles, which serves 450 kinds of beer *(see p81)*.

4 In 't Spinnekopke, Brussels
A famous old *estaminet* (traditional pub), serving a range of dishes cooked with beer *(see p75)*.

5 De Halve Maan, Bruges
A small, visitable brewery – producers of Straffe Hendrik ("Strong Henry") *(see p88)*.

6 't Brugs Beertje, Bruges
A classic beer pub, offering some 300 kinds of beer, including a range of "guest beers" on tap *(see p91)*.

7 Den Dyver, Bruges
A restaurant specializing in beer cuisine, served with fine beers *(see p92)*.

8 Le Greenwich, Brussels
A traditional pub/restaurant that was once a favourite haunt of Magritte *(see p72)*.

9 Dulle Griet, Ghent
A celebrated pub serving 250 brands of beer *(see p98)*.

10 Kulminator, Antwerp
A specialist beer bar with 500 brands, including what is claimed to be the world's strongest beer.
Vleminckveld 32 • Map T3

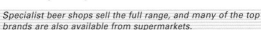

Specialist beer shops sell the full range, and many of the top brands are also available from supermarkets.

Left **Le Botanique, Brussels** Right **De Vlaamse Opera, Ghent**

Top 10 Performing Arts Venues

1 Théâtre Royal de la Monnaie, Brussels

The most revered performing arts venue in the country, La Monnaie (Dutch: De Munt) is celebrated for sparking off the Revolution of 1830 *(see p47)*, when a crowd took to the streets incited by Auber's opera *La Muette de Portici*. It was rebuilt in elegant Neo-Classical style in 1819; the interior was redesigned following a fire in 1855. La Monnaie has highly respected opera and ballet companies. *Place de la Monnaie • Map C2 • 070 23 39 39 • www.lamonnaie.be*

2 Palais des Beaux-Arts, Brussels (BOZAR)

Victor Horta's Palais des Beaux-Arts was completed in 1928. Known as BOZAR, it is a multi-arts venue, covering music, theatre, art, dance and much more. *Rue Ravenstein 23 • Map D4 • 02 507 82 00 • www.bozar.be*

3 Le Botanique, Brussels

The beautiful glasshouses of Brussels' botanical gardens were built in 1826–9. Cunning conversion of the interior has provided what is now a key venue for a wide range of cultural activities, including theatre, dance and concerts of all kinds. *Rue Royale 236, 1210 BRU (Saint-Josse-ten-Noode) • Map D1 • 02 218 37 32 • www.botanique.be*

4 Conservatoire Royal de Bruxelles, Brussels

The Brussels conservatory is a highly respected institution. Its buildings, completed in 1875, were designed by the architect of the Galeries Royales de Saint-Hubert *(see p10)*, and include a classical music venue. *Rue de la Régence 30 • Map C5 • 02 511 04 27*

5 Les Halles de Schaerbeek, Brussels

The magnificent old covered market, built in iron and glass at the end of the 19th century, has been transformed into an inspirational venue for a variety of cultural events – including drama, dance and music. *Rue Royale Sainte-Marie 22a, 1030 BRU (Schaerbeek) • Map G2 • 02 218 21 07 • www.halles.be*

6 Théâtre Royal de Toone, Brussels

The Toone marionette theatre, occupying a tiny building at the bottom of a medieval alley, is a Brussels institution. Note this is not for children: the plays – enacted by traditional puppets made of wood and papier-mâché – may be serious classics of theatre, and the language is often Bruxellois, the rich dialect of the city. *Petite Rue des Bouchers 21 (Impasse Schuddeveld 6) • Map C3 • 02 511 71 37 • www.toone.be*

Théâtre Royal de Toone

7 Concertgebouw, Bruges

As part of its celebrations as a Cultural Capital of Europe in 2002, Bruges undertook to create a new concert hall. The result is a highly innovative building that has quickly become established as a leading venue for classical music, as well as ballet and jazz. ⓢ *'t Zand 34 • Map J5 • 070 22 33 02 • www.concertgebouw.be*

8 De Vlaamse Opera, Ghent

Ghent home of the much-respected Vlaamse Opera, this classic opera house ranks among the most spectacular theatres in Europe. ⓢ *Schouwburgstraat 3 • Map Q3 • 09 268 10 11 • www.vlaamseopera.be*

De Vlaamse Opera, Antwerp

9 De Vlaamse Opera, Antwerp

Antwerp's opera house was completed in 1907, its interior elegantly decked out with marble and gilding. The Vlaamse Opera performs here and in Ghent. ⓢ *Frankrijklei 3 • Map U2 • 03 202 10 11 • www.vlaamseopera.be*

10 deSingel, Antwerp

This vibrant multi-purpose cultural centre is a venue for performances and exhibitions of drama, dance, architecture and music. ⓢ *Desguinlei 25 • 03 248 28 28 • www.desingel.be*

Top 10 Belgian Writers, Poets and Musicians

1 Roland de Lassus
Also known as Orlando di Lasso (c.1532–94). One of the leading composers of his day.

2 César Franck
Organist and composer (1822–90) in the Romantic tradition.

3 Émile Verhaeren
Symbolist poet (1855–1916) noted for his portrayals (in French) of Flanders.

4 Maurice Maeterlinck
Nobel-Prize-winning Symbolist poet and dramatist (1862–1949).

5 Michel de Ghelderode
Belgium's most celebrated 20th-century playwright (1898–1962), and one of the most original writers in the French language.

6 Georges Simenon
Prolific master of the popular detective story (1903–89) and creator of Inspector Maigret *(see p48)*.

7 Django Reinhardt
The most celebrated of all jazz guitarists, Reinhardt (1910–53) was a key member of the renowned Quintet of the Hot Club of France.

8 Arthur Grumiaux
A leading violinist of his era (1921–86).

9 Hugo Claus
Belgium's most revered writer (1929–2008), a Bruges-born poet, playwright and novelist.

10 Amélie Nothomb
One of Belgium's most successful modern novelists (born 1967), noted for her exploration of the darker sides of human nature.

Left **Butte de Lion, Waterloo** Right **Forêt de Soignes**

Top 10 Excursions

1 Waterloo

Among the fields and farmhouses near Waterloo, 15 km (9 miles) south of Brussels, Napoleon was finally defeated. The battlefield has been a tourist site virtually since the battle itself. The modern Visitor Centre, next to the Butte de Lion mound, is a good place to start. *Route du Lion 315, 1410 Waterloo • www.waterloo1815.be • Open 9:30am–6:30pm daily (Oct–Mar: 10am–5pm) • Adm charge*

2 Walibi Belgium

Belgium's biggest and best-known theme park – a good day out for the kids *(see p52)*.

3 Forêt de Soignes

The magnificent ancient beech forests of Soignes provide a splendid landscape for walking or cycling – particularly in autumn, when the beech trees turn golden. There are two arboretums, at Groenendaal and Tervuren, and an information centre on the site of the 14th-century Abbaye de Rouge-Cloître. *Drève du Rouge-Cloître 4 • www.soignes-zonien.net*

Namur

4 Namur

An attractive town on the confluence of the Rivers Meuse and Sambre, Namur is famous above all for its mighty Citadelle (open Jun–Sep), perched dramatically on a steep-sided hill. *Tourist Office: Square Léopold • 081 24 64 49 • www.namurtourisme.be*

5 Leuven

The old university town of Leuven (French: Louvain) has a deep charm, derived from its compact human scale and many historic buildings – chief among them the Stadhuis, the most beautiful Gothic town hall of them all. *Tourist Office: Naamsestraat 3 • 016 20 30 20 • www.leuven.be*

6 Mechelen

Mechelen (French: Malines) was a proud trading city in the Burgundian era, and centre of power under Margaret of Austria (1507–30). Dominating the city is the vast bell-tower of Sint-Romboutskathedraal – originally intended to be twice as high. *Tourist Office: Hallestraat 2–4 • 070 22 00 08 • www.toerismemechelen.be*

7 Ostend

Ostend (spelt Oostende locally) is famous as a resort and for its excellent seafood. It also has surprisingly good collections of art, in the Provinciaal Museum voor Moderne Kunst and the Museum voor Schone Kunsten. *Tourist Office: Monacoplein 2 • 059 70 11 99 • www.visitoostende.be*

Waterloo, Six Flags Belgium, the Fôret de Soignes, Namur, Leuven, Mechelen and Lier can all be easily reached from Brussels.

8 Lier

This charming little town to the south-east of Antwerp has a handsome collection of historic buildings clustered around the Grote Markt, but its most famous possession is the Zimmertoren, a 14th-century watch-tower with the fascinating Centenary Clock. *Tourist Office: Grote Markt 57 • 038 00 05 55 • www.toerismelier.be*

9 Damme

A pretty cluster of late-medieval buildings is all that remains of the once-prosperous town at the head of the canal to Bruges. A pleasant excursion by bus or bicycle. *Tourist Office: Huyse de Grote Sterre, Jacob van Maerlantstraat 3 • 050 28 86 10 • www.toerismedamme.be*

10 Ieper (Ypres)

Ieper (French: Ypres) was one of the great medieval trading cities of Flanders. Its historic past was all but erased when it became the focal point of bitter trench warfare in World War I. Today it is the centre for visits to the trenches and the many cemeteries, and site of the Menin Gate, the memorial arch marking the road along which so many soldiers marched, never to return. But the real draw is "In Flanders Fields", a superb museum depicting the background and course of the war, its experiences, textures and horrors – a richly informative and deeply moving experience. *In Flanders Fields: Lakenhallen, Grote Markt 34 • 057 23 92 20 • www.toerismeieper.be; www.inflandersfields.be • Open Apr–mid-Nov: 10am–6pm daily; mid-Nov–Mar: 10am–5pm Tue–Sun. Closed 3 weeks in Jan • Adm charge*

In Flanders Fields, Ieper (Ypres)

Centenary Clock, Lier

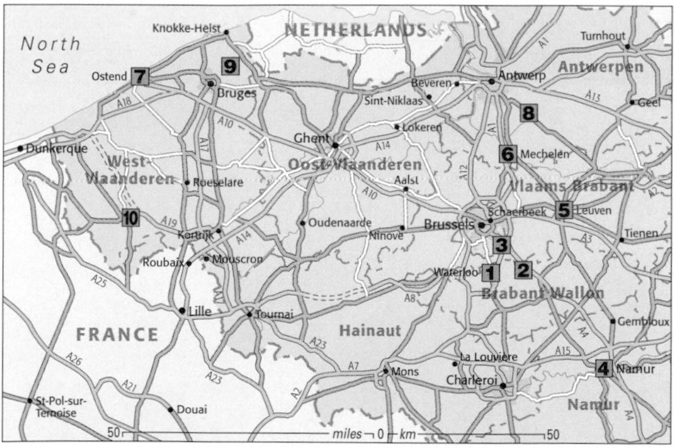

Ostend and Damme are short journeys from Bruges. Ieper (Ypres) is most conveniently visited from Bruges or Ghent.

AROUND BRUSSELS, BRUGES, ANTWERP & GHENT

Left **Place du Petit Sablon** Right **Grand Place**

Central Brussels

THE CENTRE OF BRUSSELS IS NEATLY CONTAINED *within a clearly defined shape called the Pentagon. Nowadays this outline is formed by a busy ring road called the Petite Ceinture. The road follows the path of the old city walls, a huge 14th-century construction 9 km (6 miles) long. Few traces of the walls have survived, but one old city gate, the Porte de Hal, still stands, and gives a fair indication of just how massive the fortifications must have been. Most of historic Brussels is contained within these bounds, including both the commercial and popular districts of the Lower Town, and the aristocratic quarter of the Upper Town, which includes the Royal Palace. The result is that Brussels is a very compact city. You can walk right across the Pentagon in about half an hour. As well as monuments and cultural gems, you will find a concentration of excellent places to stay and eat, good shops, and vibrant cafés and bars.*

Tintin and Snowy

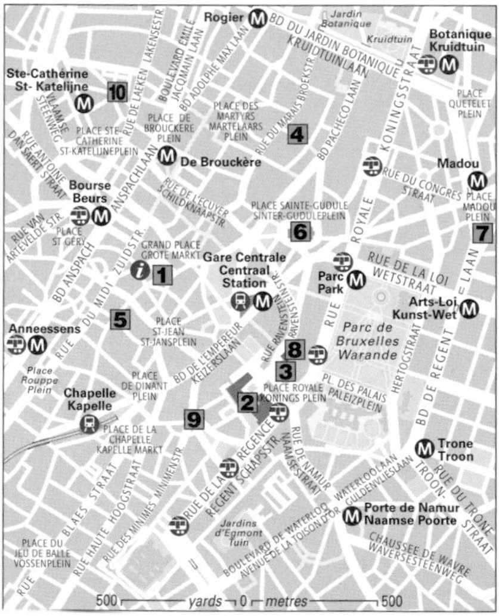

Sights

1. Grand Place
2. Musées Royaux des Beaux-Arts
3. Musée des Instruments de Musique
4. Centre Belge de la Bande Dessinée
5. Manneken-Pis
6. Cathédrale des Saints Michel et Gudule
7. Musée Charlier
8. Palais Coudenberg
9. Sablon
10. Église Saint-Jean-Baptiste au Béguinage

Preceding pages **Brabo Fountain, Grote Markt, Antwerp**

1 Grand Place

No trip to Brussels would be complete without a visit to the Grand Place – even if it's just to stock up on some Belgian biscuits or chocolates. A remarkable legacy of the city's Gothic and Renaissance past, it is also a monument to the values and ingenuity of the artisans and merchants who were the architects of Brussels' prosperity *(see pp8–9)*.

Manneken-Pis

2 Musées Royaux des Beaux-Arts

This is a superb, "must-see" collection, notable because it focuses almost exclusively on Flemish and Belgian art. Highlights include rare works by Pieter Brueghel the Elder, the exhilarating Rubens collection, and an unparalleled assembly of works by the Belgian Symbolists, as well as the Magritte Museum showcasing an extensive collection *(see pp12–15)*.

3 Musée des Instruments de Musique

The famous "mim" collection of historical and contemporary musical instruments is housed in the remarkable Art Nouveau department store known as "Old England". Take the children too: a visitor guidance system brings the exhibits to life by letting visitors hear what the instruments sound like when played *(see pp16–17)*.

4 Centre Belge de la Bande Dessinée

Reflecting the huge popularity of comic-strip books in Belgium – and, indeed, most of continental Europe – this unique "Belgian Centre of the Comic Strip" is a shrine to the art form. Archive material and other exhibits focus above all on Belgian contributors to the genre – most notably, of course, on Hergé, the creator of Tintin *(see pp20–21)*.

5 Manneken-Pis

In Brussels you can't avoid this cheeky little chap, famously pissing with carefree abandon just as little boys do. Among other things, he's on postcards, T-shirts, key rings and corkscrews. So why not take a pilgrimage to see the real thing – a tiny bronze statue – and bask in the happy absurdity of it all? It must be worth a photograph *(see p10)*.

Le Ruisseau **by Léon Frédéric, Musées Royaux des Beaux-Arts**

For Brussels tourist information **See p112**

6 Cathédrale des Saints Michel et Gudule

Brussels' largest and finest church was built from 1226 onwards and showcases over 300 years' worth of architectural design. Highlights inside include an enormous Baroque oak pulpit, splendid Renaissance stained-glass windows, and access to the treasury and preserved remnants of the old Romanesque church that once stood here. Dedicated to St Michael, patron saint of the city, the cathedral's name also acknowledges St Gudule, a local 8th-century saint who outfoxed the Devil. The cathedral is often used for

Cathédrale des Saints Michel et Gudule

ceremonies of national interest, such as royal weddings and state funerals. *Parvis Sainte-Gudule • Map D3 • 02 217 83 45 • Open 7am–6pm Mon–Fri, 8:30am–3:30pm Sat, 2pm–6pm Sun. • Admission charges only for Museum of Church Treasures and Crypt*

7 Musée Charlier

Brussels is a city of grand old 19th-century mansions, or *maisons de maître*. This museum provides a rare opportunity to see inside one. The original owner, Henri van Curtsem, commissioned Victor Horta *(see p49)* to redesign the interior. In the hands of van Curtsem's adoptive heir, sculptor Guillaume Charlier, the mansion became a centre for Brussels' avant-garde. On his death in 1925, Charlier left the house to the city, and it retains much of the decor of his era. There are works by leading artists of the time, such as James Ensor, Léon Frédéric, Fernand Khnopff and Rik Wouters, plus an impressive collection of antique furniture. *Avenue des Arts 16 • Map E3 • 02 220 26 91 • www.charliermuseum.be • Open noon–5pm Mon–Thu, 10am–1pm Fri • Adm charge*

8 Palais Coudenberg

Accessed via the Musée Belvue *(see p70)*, this staggering archaeological site was once the medieval Coudenberg Palace that stood on Place Royale. The palace was the seat of residence for the Duchy of Brabant and then the Governors of the Netherlands for more than 600 years until it burned down in 1731. The highlight is the impressive Aula Magna banqueting hall, which was the scene of Charles V's abdication in 1555. *Place des Palais 7 • Map D4 • 070 22 04 92 • Open 10am–5pm Tue–Fri, 10am–6pm Sat & Sun • Adm charge*

The Pentagon

The first city walls to enclose Brussels were built in about 1100 but the city expanded and they were superseded in 1381, creating the neat pentagon shape that is evident today. These walls were eventually knocked down in the mid-19th century to make way for tree-lined boulevards. Of the city gates, only the Porte de Hal remains.

For more Brussels churches See pp42–3

Sablon antiques market, Brussels

9 Sablon

The name Sablon refers to the sandy marshland that occupied this site until it was reclaimed in the 17th century. The Place du Grand Sablon is a centre for antiques and is home to two of Brussels' leading chocolate makers: Wittamer and Pierre Marcolini. Look out for the statue of Tintin too. The Place du Petit Sablon park is adorned with 48 statues of the medieval guilds of Brussels. Separating the two is the Église Notre-Dame du Sablon. *Rue de la Régence 3B • Map C4 • Open 8am–6pm Mon–Fri, 9:30am–6pm Sat, 10am–6pm Sun • Free*

10 Église St-Jean-Baptiste au Béguinage

Considered to be one of the prettiest churches in Belgium, this Baroque beauty belonged to a *béguinage* (institution for pious women) and dates from the 17th century. Note the tombstones of the *béguines* set in the floor. *Place du Béguinage • Map B1 • 02 217 87 42 • Open 10am–5pm Tue–Sat, 10am–8pm Sun • Free*

A Day in the Centre

Morning

Start off with the essentials: a stroll around the **Grand Place** *(see pp8–9)* and a trip to the **Manneken-Pis** *(see p10)*, stopping for a waffle at the Dandoy shop at 14 Rue Charles Buls on the way. Now head back to the Bourse *(see p10)*, and go west along Rue Dansaert, the street for cutting-edge fashion. Turn right at the Rue du Vieux Marché aux Grains and walk up to the **Église Sainte-Catherine,** a church designed in 1854 by Joseph Poelaert, who was also responsible for the colossal Palais de Justice. It stands on reclaimed land at the head of a canal now covered over by the Place Sainte-Catherine. This was the site of the old fish market, and is still famous for its fish restaurants. It could be the place to stop for a spot of lunch.

Afternoon

Walk back east, stopping at the **Cathédrale des Saints Michel et Gudule** before heading up the hill to Rue Royale. Take a stroll in the pleasant **Park de Bruxelles,** then walk south to the **Palais Royal** *(see p70)* and the elegant 17th-century Place Royale, with its statue of the 11th-century crusader Godefroy de Bouillon. You're now a stone's throw from both the **Musées Royaux des Beaux-Arts** and the **Musée des Instruments de Musique** *(see p67)*. Take your pick. After this, you'll probably need some refreshments, so continue down the Rue de la Régence to the cafés and chocolate shops of the **Sablon** district.

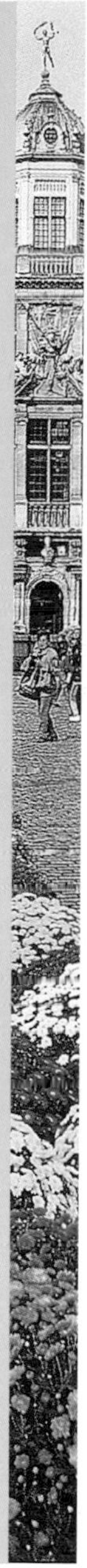

Left **Palais Royal** Right **Église Notre-Dame de la Chapelle**

TOP 10 Best of the Rest

1 Galeries Royales de Saint-Hubert

When it opened in 1847, this elegant shopping arcade was the grandest in Europe *(see p10)*.

2 Musée du Costume et de la Dentelle

Exquisite examples of costume and lace, an industry that employed 10,000 women in mid-19th-century Brussels *(see p10)*.

3 Place des Martyrs

The 445 "martyrs" killed in the Belgian Revolution of 1830 lie buried in this square. *Map C2*

4 Église Notre-Dame de la Chapelle

This large, atmospheric church is like something out of a Brueghel painting – aptly so, since Pieter Brueghel the Elder is buried here. *Place de la Chapelle • Map B4 • Open Nov–Feb: 9am–6pm daily, Mar–Oct: 9am–7pm daily • Free*

5 Palais Royal and Musée Belvue

See how the other half lived in the grand rooms of the Royal Palace. A former hotel next to the palace houses a museum devoted to the history of Belgium since 1830. *Place des Palais. Map D4 • Palais Royal: 02 551 20 20. Open Jul–mid-Sep: 10:30am–4:30pm Tue–Sun. Free • Musée Belvue: 070 22 04 92. Open 10am–5pm Tue–Fri, 10am–6pm Sat & Sun • Adm charge*

6 Palais de Charles de Lorraine

This suite of 18th-century rooms contains a small but select exhibition of furniture, porcelain, clocks and other artifacts. *Place du Musée 1 • Map C4 • Open 1–5pm Wed & Sat (closed Sat in Jul & Aug) • Adm charge*

7 Cinematek

A bijou cinema with a fascinating collection tracing the early history of the moving image in the foyer. *Rue Baron Horta 9 • Map D4 • 02 551 19 00 • Open daily • Adm charge*

8 Porte de Hal

The sole surviving gate of the 14th-century city walls. *Boulevard du Midi 150 • Map B6 • 02 534 34 50 • Open 9:30am–5pm Tue–Fri; 10am–5pm Sat & Sun • Adm charge (free first Wed of month)*

9 Palais de Justice

There is something gloriously megalomaniac about this vast Neo-Classical pile. *Place Poelaert • Map B5 • Open 9am–3pm Mon–Fri • Free*

10 Musée du Jouet

This delightful toy museum appeals to everyone. *Rue de l'Association 24 • Map E2 • 02 219 61 68 • Open 10am–noon & 2–6pm daily • Adm charge*

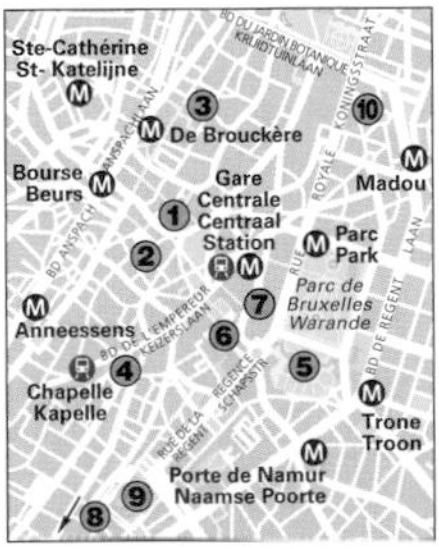

Left **Galerie Bortier** Right **Galeries Royales de Saint-Hubert**

Top 10 Shopping

1 Galeries Royales de Saint-Hubert
A spectacularly elegant and spacious shopping arcade built in 1847 *(see p10)*.

2 Rue Neuve
A pedestrianized shopping street close to the city centre, with many of the main European fashion chains and a large Inno department store at the northern end. *Map C1*

3 Rue Antoine Dansaert
Ignore the shoddy environs: this is the place for cutting-edge fashion. All the Antwerp designers are represented in the shops here, and there are several outlets for notable Belgian fashion labels. *Map B2*

4 Galerie Bortier
Smaller than the Galeries Royales de Saint-Hubert, but just as elegant. Here you'll find second-hand books, prints, postcards and posters. *Map C3*

5 Place du Grand Sablon
There are antique shops fronting onto the square, but try poking around in some of the side passages as well. Two of the finest chocolatiers, Wittamer and Marcolini, are here *(see p55)*. *Map C4*

6 Avenue and Galerie Louise
Top-name international couturiers, including Chanel, Hermes and Christian Dior, line Avenue Louise, while Congolese clothes shops, hairdressers and jewellers can be found in the covered Galerie Louise. *Map C5*

7 Galerie de la Toison d'Or
This covered arcade, similar to Galerie Louise, offers a good range of stores close to the Porte de Namur. *Map D5*

8 Christmas Market
From early December to early January, this market offers all things Christmassy – crafts, decorations, presents – in the streets around the Bourse and on Quai aux Briques. *Map B3*

9 Rue Blaes and Place du Jeu de Balle
The Place du Jeu de Balle has a daily flea market (6am–2pm) selling antiques, junk and curios, and there is a spread of shops up Rue Blaes too. *Map B5*

10 Galerie Agora
This maze-like covered arcade sells T-shirts, baseball caps, leather goods, costume jewellery and incense – all surprisingly in the lower price range. *Map C3*

Visit the Place du Grand Sablon for the weekend antiques market.

Left **Wittamer** Right **Café du Vaudeville**

TOP 10 Bars and Cafés

1 Le Roy d'Espagne

A famous watering-hole in the old bakers' guildhouse. There is a medieval air to the interior decor. Also serves light meals. ✆ *Grand Place 1 • Map C3*

2 Au Bon Vieux Temps

Blink and you'll miss this 17th-century tavern tucked down a side street of Rue du Marché aux Herbes. A great spot for people watching. ✆ *Impasse St-Nicolas 4 • Map C3*

3 Café du Vaudeville

Not many cafés can claim to have had Marx, Rodin and Victor Hugo among their clientele, but the Vaudeville has a long history. Sit outside in the city's most splendid arcade, or upstairs in a salon decorated with copies of the Communist Manifesto. ✆ *Galerie de la Reine 11 • Map C3*

4 A La Mort Subite

"Sudden Death" may sound alarming, but this famous bar, redesigned in Rococo style in 1926, is named after a card game. It is also the name of a *gueuze* beer *(see pp58–9)*. ✆ *Rue Montagne aux Herbes Potagères 7 • Map C2*

5 La Cirio

Another classic, Le Cirio has been open since 1886 and is famous for its *half-en-half* – a mix of still and sparkling white wine. ✆ *Rue de la Bourse 18 • Map B3*

6 Falstaff

Situated opposite La Bourse *(see p10)*, Falstaff is a Brussels institution thanks to its stunning 1903 Art Nouveau design. Lively atmosphere and efficient, polite service. ✆ *Rue Henri Maus 19–25 • Map B3*

7 Le Greenwich

An established Brussels favourite, especially popular with an avid chess-playing crowd. It was a former hang-out of Magritte. ✆ *Rue des Chartreux 7 • Map B2*

8 Wittamer

The world-class chocolatier has seating where you can sample its heavenly products with a cup of tea or coffee. ✆ *Place du Grand Sablon 12–13 • Map C4*

9 mim

The Musée des Instruments de Musique's spectacular roof-top café *(see pp16–17)*. ✆ *Rue Montagne de la Cour 2 • Map D4*

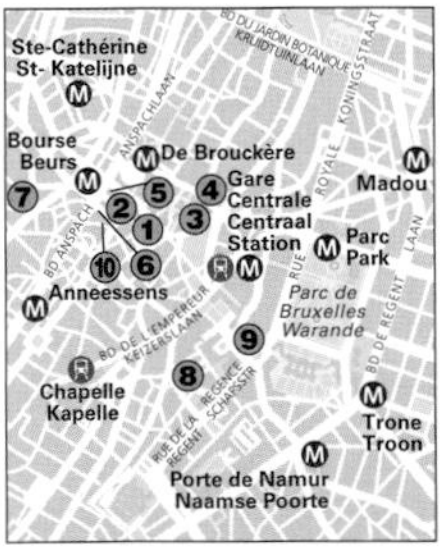

10 Bonnefooi

This lively bar draws a young crowd with its live music on week nights and DJs at the weekend. Great atmosphere especially in summer. ✆ *Steenstraat/Rue des Pierres 8 • Map B3*

Left **The Music Village** Right **Archiduc**

Top 10 Brussels Nightlife

1 Archiduc
This legendary 1930s Art Deco bar – designed to evoke a cruise liner – has entertained all the jazz greats. The place picks up after midnight. *Rue Antoine Dansaert 6–8 • Map B2 • 02 512 06 52*

2 Blaes 208
Behind the gritty industrial exterior lies the best disco in town. World-class DJs spin a mix of techno and drum'n' bass. *Rue Blaes 208 • Map B5 • 02 511 97 89*

3 Club Avenue
A glitzy Upper Town nightclub where international funk and groove mixes with cutting-edge French rap and R&B artists. *Avenue de la Toison d'Or 44 • Map C6 • www.studio44.be*

4 Le Bazaar
It's hard to miss this stylish club, which hosts world music and dance parties most Friday and Saturday nights. International DJs also play here. *Rue des Capucins 63 • Map B5 • 02 511 26 00*

5 The Music Village
Jazz and blues bar with live concerts every night: 8:30pm on weeknights; 9pm on weekends. Dinner is available either before or during the performances. *Rue des Pierres 50 • Map B3 • 02 513 50 52*

6 Spirito Martini
Housed in a former Anglican church, this swish nightclub/ restaurant features a sumptuous gold and crystal decor, beautiful lighting and a vast dancefloor. *Rue Stassart 18 • Map C6 • 02 502 30 00*

7 The Wood
Take a taxi to the city's trendiest watering hole in a renovated hunting lodge set amid the trees of the enchanting Bois de la Cambre. Terrace in summer. *Avenue de Flore 3–5 • Map C6*

8 Le You
This popular club enjoys a lively central location. The music ranges from electro and house to 1980s retro and R&B. On Sundays, Le You attracts a predominantly gay crowd. *Rue Duquesnoy 18 • Map C3 • 02 639 14 00*

9 The Flat
At this townhouse lounge bar you can sip your cocktail in the lounge, bedroom or bathroom! *Rue de la Reinette 12 • Map D5*

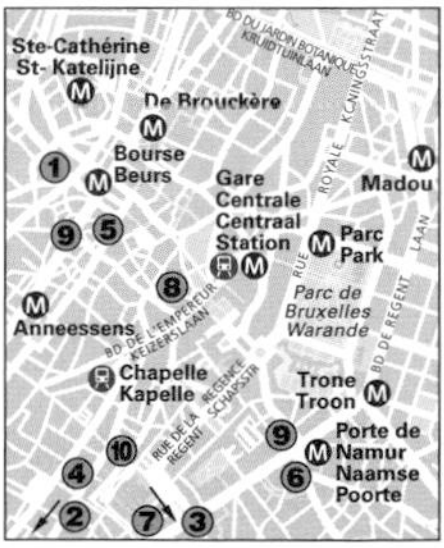

10 Havana
The ambience may be Latin but the music comes in all varieties at this lively dance club. Open late Thursday and all night at weekends. Four bars, restaurant. *Rue de l'Épée 4 • Map B5 • 02 502 12 24*

Left **Belga Queen** Right **Comme Chez Soi**

Top 10 Restaurants

1 Comme Chez Soi

Brussels' most celebrated restaurant is family run and has two Michelin stars. For a taste of the superlative, innovative French cuisine, be sure to book weeks ahead. *Place Rouppe 23 • Map B4 • 02 512 29 21 • Closed Wed L, Sun, Mon, mid-Jul–mid-Aug • €€€€€*

2 L'Ecailler du Palais Royal

One of Brussels' most prestigious fish restaurants, this quiet, refined establishment attracts a mature clientele. *Rue Bodenbroeck 18 • Map C4 • 02 512 87 51 • Closed Sun, Aug • €€€€€*

3 Belga Queen

A stylish restaurant housed in an ornate former bank. The French-Belgian menu offers better value at lunchtime. *Rue du Fossé-aux-Loups 32 • Map C2 • 02 217 21 87 • €€€€€*

4 Kwint

Dine on first-class fish and pasta beneath a world-renowned Arne Quinze sculpture at this elegant restaurant. *Mont des Arts 1 • Map C4 • 02 505 95 95 • Closed Sun • €€€€€*

5 Sea Grill, SAS Radisson

Boasting two Michelin stars, this fish restaurant offers refined dining. *Rue du Fossé-aux-Loups 47 • Map C2 • 02 218 08 00 • Closed Sat, Sun • €€€€€*

6 La Belle Maraîchère

A favourite with locals for three decades, this timeless wood-panelled restaurant serves top-rate fish dishes. *Place Sainte-Catherine 11a • Map B2 • 02 512 97 59 • Closed Wed, Thu • €€€€€*

7 Cospaia

This sleek, sexy restaurant on the southern edge of the Pentagon serves fusion cuisine. During the day, opt for the white dining room; at night, the black room is more romantic. *Captaine Crespel 1 • Map C5 • 02 513 03 03 • Closed Sat L, Sun • €€€€*

8 L'Idiot du Village

A long-standing favourite with locals who consistently praise the inventive menus and romantic shabby-chic style. *Rue Notre-Seigneur 29 • Map B4 • 02 502 55 82 • Closed Sat, Sun • €€€*

9 Aux Armes de Bruxelles

Founded in 1921, Aux Armes de Bruxelles is an institution: white-linen elegance and impeccable Belgian cooking. *Rue des Bouchers 13 • Map C3 • 02 511 55 50 • €€€*

10 Restaurant Vincent

Dine on mussels and flambéed steaks in a room decorated with old marine murals. *Rue des Dominicains 8–10 • Map C3 • 02 511 26 07 • €€€*

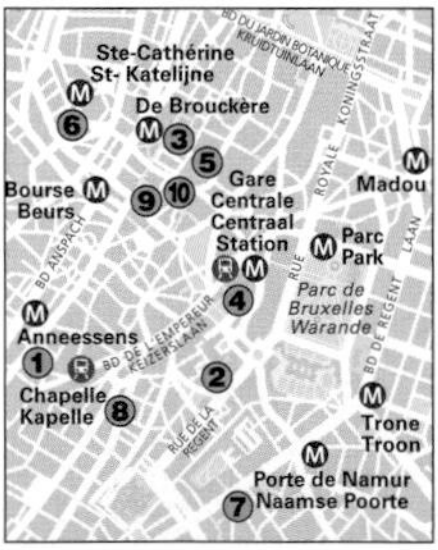

Note: *Most Brussels residents avoid the tourist restaurants in the Rue des Bouchers.*

'**t Kelderke**

Price Categories

For a three-course meal for one with half a bottle of wine (or equivalent meal), taxes and extra charges.	€ under €30 €€ €30–€40 €€€ €40–€50 €€€€ €50–€60 €€€€€ over €60

TOP 10 Lunch Spots, Brasseries & Bistros

1 Cap d'Argent

A no-frills bistro admired for its tasty Belgian classics and first-rate service. *Rue Ravenstein 10 • Map D3 • 02 513 09 19 • Closed Sun • €€*

2 In 't Spinnekopke

An appealing *estaminet* (traditional pub) that stands by its 18th-century heritage to present a menu of fine Belgian-Bruxellois dishes. *Place du Jardin-aux-Fleurs 1 • Map A3 • 02 511 86 95 • Closed Sat L, Sun • €€*

3 Bozar Brasserie

Designed by Victor Horta in 1928, this Art Deco gem is in beautiful condition after a loving renovation. The Michelin-starred chef prepares faultless Belgian cuisine. *Rue Baron Horta 3 • Map D3 • 02 503 00 00 • Closed Sun, Mon • €€€€*

4 Les Petits Oignons

Treat yourself to a fancy lunch at this elegant brasserie, which receives glowing reviews. The carefully selected wine list also contributes to the restaurant's popularity. *Rue de la Régence 25 • Map C5 • 02 511 76 15 • €€€*

5 Le Crachin

A jovial café serving sweet and savoury traditional Breton pancakes with mugs of Brittany cider. *Rue de Flandre 12 • Map B2 • 02 502 13 00 • €*

6 Le Pain Quotidien

Selling excellent bread with delicious fillings, as well as tempting pastries, Le Pain Quotidien ("Daily Bread") is a huge success. This is the most central of the many city branches. *Rue Antoine Dansaert 16a • Map B2 • 02 502 23 61 • €*

7 Chez Patrick

This cherished and popular restaurant refuses to change or diverge from its traditions of solid, good-value, truly Belgian cooking. *Rue des Chapeliers 6 • Map C3 • 02 511 98 15 • Closed Sun, Mon • €€€*

8 Taverne du Passage

A traditional 1930s Belgian diner with accomplished waiters and an enthusiastic local clientele. The fish dishes are excellent. *Galerie de la Reine 30 • Map C3 • 02 512 37 31 • €€€*

9 't Kelderke

A 17th-century cellar-restaurant delivering feasts of Belgian cuisine. The good food attracts appreciative locals as well as tourists. *Grand Place 15 • Map C3 • 02 513 73 44 • €€*

10 Chez Léon

Established in 1893, this *moules-frites* specialist is now an international brand. *Rue des Bouchers 18 • Map C3 • 02 511 14 15 • €€*

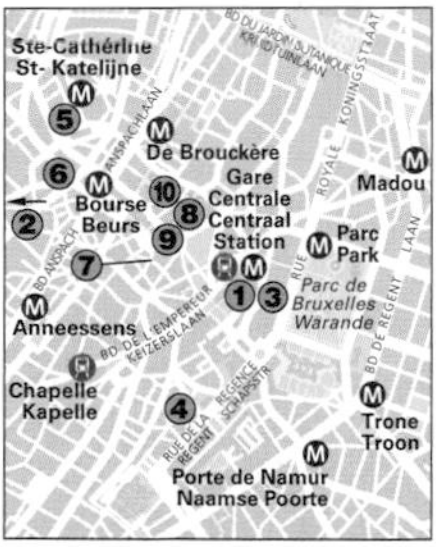

Left **Autoworld** Right **Musée Royal de l'Armée et d'Histoire Militaire**

Outer Brussels

OVER THE CENTURIES, BRUSSELS EXPANDED *beyond the old city walls, gradually absorbing neighbouring towns and villages. These outlying communes – such as Ixelles, Saint-Gilles and Anderlecht – still retain their distinctive characters. As a result, there is huge variety across Outer Brussels. An excellent public transport system makes it easy to scoot around these suburbs, and the highlights listed here are definitely worth the journey.*

TOP 10 Sights

1. **Parc du Cinquantenaire**
2. **Musée Horta**
3. **Musée David et Alice van Buuren**
4. **Pavillon Chinois and Tour Japonaise**
5. **The Atomium**
6. **Musée du Tram Bruxellois**
7. **Parlement Européen and the Parlementarium**
8. **Musée Communal d'Ixelles**
9. **Musée Constantin Meunier**
10. **Musée Antoine Wiertz**

Tour Japonaise

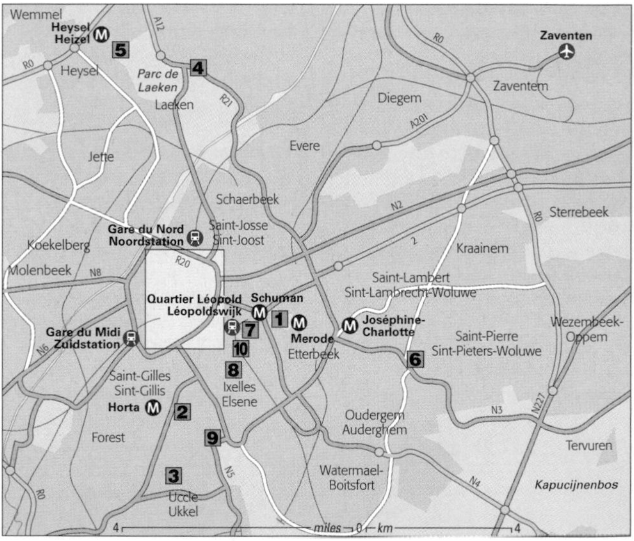

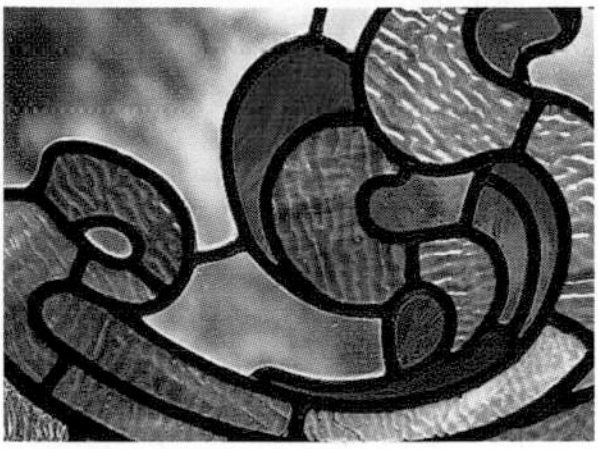

Musée Horta

1 Parc du Cinquantenaire

In 1880 King Léopold II staged a grand international fair to celebrate the 50th anniversary of the founding of his nation. The vast exhibition halls he erected, together with their successors, now contain a cluster of major museums. By far the most spectacular is the Musées Royaux d'Art et d'Histoire, a rich collection of treasures from around the world, including archaeological finds, anthropological artifacts and decorative arts. Close by are the Musée Royal de l'Armée et d'Histoire Militaire (an extensive military museum) and Autoworld (a major collection of historic cars). The park also contains the extraordinary Atelier de Moulage *(see p41)*, and the Pavillon Horta, a Neo-Classical work designed by a young Victor Horta to house an erotic sculpture by Jef Lambeaux (1852–1908). *Map H4 • Musées Royaux d'Art et d'Histoire: Parc du Cinquantenaire 10. 02 741 72 11. www.kmkg-mrah.be. Open 9:30am–5pm Tue–Fri, 10am–5pm Sat–Sun. Closed Mon and public hols. Adm charge (free 1–5pm 1st Wed of month) • Musée Royal de l'Armée: Parc du Cinquantaire 3. 02 737 78 11. www.klm-mra.be. Open 9am–noon, 1–4:45pm. Closed Mon and public hols. Free • Autoworld: Parc du Cinquantenaire 11. 02 736 41 65. www.autoworld.be. Open Apr–Sep: 10am–6pm daily; Oct–Mar: 10am–5pm daily. Adm charge*

2 Musée Horta

A symphony in Art Nouveau design *(see pp18–19)*.

3 Musée David et Alice van Buuren

This beautifully preserved Art Deco home has excellent furniture and stained glass, as well as contemporary paintings. *Ave Léo Errera 41, 1180 BRU (Uccle) • Map G3 • 02 343 48 51 • www.museumvanbuuren.com • Museum & garden open 2–5:30pm daily • Adm charge*

4 Pavillon Chinois and Tour Japonaise

Another legacy of King Léopold, the Chinese Pavilion and Japanese Tower now house porcelain, samurai armour and Art Nouveau stained glass. Nearby is the Museum of Japanese Art. *Ave Van Praet 44, 1020 BRU (Laeken) • Map G1 • 02 268 16 08 • www.kmkg-mrah.be • Open 9:30am–5pm Tue–Fri, 10am–5pm Sat & Sun • Adm charge*

5 The Atomium

This giant model of an iron crystal was built as Belgium's exhibit at Brussels' 1958 Universal Exposition. *Square de l'Atomium, 1020 BRU (Laeken) • Map F1 (inset) • 02 475 47 75 • www.atomium.be • Open 10am–6pm daily • Adm charge*

The Atomium

Be sure to see the medieval church treasures in the Salle aux Trésors of the Musées Royaux d'Art et d'Histoire

Musée du Tram Bruxellois

6 Musée du Tram Bruxellois

The trams of modern Brussels are the last vestiges of a transport system that has formed an integral part of the city's character. Visitors cannot fail to be won over by this extensive collection of over 60 trams, from the horse-drawn "hippomobiles" of the 1860s to sleek expressions of 1960s modernity, all housed in an old tram depot. You can also enjoy a 20-minute ride on a historic tram to (and from) Tervuren (and the Africa Museum) or the Parc Cinquantenaire. *Ave de Tervuren 364B, 1150 BRU (Woluwe-Saint-Pierre) • Map G2 • 02 515 31 08/10 • www.trammuseumbrussels.be • Open 1st weekend Apr–1st weekend Oct: 1–7pm Sat, Sun and public hols • Adm charge (additional charge for ride on historic tram)*

7 Parlement Européen and the Parlamentarium

EU politics may seem a dry, complex issue, but a trip to the European Parliament and its visitor centre will convince you otherwise. Free audio-guided tours of the Parliament are available, while the Parlamentarium explains the past, present and future of the EU in more detail. Visitors to the Parlamentarium are provided with a multimedia handset, which guides them around the interactive displays. Meet the MEPs who shape European laws, listen to the multitude of EU languages in the Tunnel of Voices, and find out why the Parliament decamps from Brussels to Strasbourg every year. *Rue Wiertz 60, 1047 BRU • Map F5 • 02 283 22 22 • www.europarl.europa.eu • Audio tour open 10am & 3pm Mon–Thu, 10am Fri • Parlamentarium open 1am–6pm Mon, 9am–8pm Tue–Wed, 9am–6pm Thu & Fri, 10am–5pm Sat & Sun • Free*

8 Musée d'Ixelles

It's well worth the trek to this southern suburb for this small but unusually choice municipal art collection. It has a number of minor works by great masters, including Rembrandt, Delacroix and Picasso, as well as an excellent collection of posters by Toulouse-Lautrec. This is also a good place to see more work by Symbolists such as Léon Spilliaert and Léon Frédéric, and the much-cherished sculpture and Fauve-style painting of Rik Wouters. *Rue J Van Volsem 71, 1050 BRU (Ixelles) • Map E6 • 02 515 64 21 • www.museumofixelles.irisnet.be • Open 9:30am–5pm Tue–Sun. Closed Mon and public hols • Free (except during exhibitions)*

King Léopold II

Belgium's second king reigned from 1865 to 1909, a time of great change in Europe. Léopold II was an enthusiast of modernization, and undertook many grand building projects. Determined to make Belgium a colonial power, he created and ruled the Belgian Congo. However, his regime there was brutal, and millions of deaths occurred under his reign.

9 Musée Constantin Meunier

Constantin Meunier (1831–1905) was one of the great sculptors of the late 19th century, internationally famous for his instantly recognizable bronzes of working people – especially *puddleurs* (forge workers). The museum occupies his former home, and contains excellent examples of his work. *Rue de l'Abbaye 59, 1050 BRU (Ixelles) • Map G2 • 02 648 44 49 • www.fine-arts-museum.be • Open 10am–noon, 1–5pm Tue–Fri. Closed Mon, weekends and public hols • Free*

Musée Antoine Wiertz

10 Musée Antoine Wiertz

This is one of the most extraordinary museums in Brussels. Antoine Wiertz (1806–65) was an artist whose self-esteem far outstripped his talent. As a young man, he was egged on by patrons, and success went to his head. This grand studio was built so he could paint works on a scale to rival Michelangelo. The grandiose canvases are interesting in themselves, but so too are the smaller works, many so macabre and moralistic they inspire wonderment and mirth. *Rue Vautier 62, 1050 BRU (Ixelles) • Map F5 • 02 648 17 18 • www.fine-arts-museum.be • Open 10am–noon, 1–5pm Tue–Fri. Closed Mon, public hols and Sat–Sun (except for pre-booked groups) • Free*

A Walk through the Brussels of Léopold II

Morning

Put on your best walking shoes, because you're going to cover at least 5 km (3 miles) of pavement and take in half a dozen museums. You don't have to do them all, of course, and don't try this on a Monday, when most of the museums are closed. Start at the Schuman métro station in the heart of the European Quarter, close to the Justus Lipsius Building. If you're feeling energetic, stride up Rue Archimède to admire the weirdest Art Nouveau building of them all – the **Hôtel Saint-Cyr** in Square Ambiorix *(see p44)*. Otherwise, head into the **Parc du Cinquantenaire** *(see p77)* and take your pick of the museums. To refresh yourself, go to **Place Jourdan**, where there are numerous cafés and restaurants to suit all pockets.

Afternoon

Cross the Parc Léopold to visit the wacky **Musée Wiertz** *(see left)*, then walk about 1 km (1000 yd) to the delightful **Musée d'Ixelles** *(see opposite)*. If you've had enough already, you could slink into the trendy **Café Belga** in the 1930s Flagey radio building *(see p81)*; otherwise, push on down the Chaussée de Vleurgat to the **Musée Constantin Meunier** *(see above left)*. Now you're only 10 minutes away from the **Musée Horta** *(see pp18–19)*. From here you can get a tram home, or wander around the Art Nouveau houses in the vicinity *(see pp44–5)* and finish the day at the popular **Belgo Belge** *(see p81)*.

For more on Belgian artists **See pp36–7**

Left **Basilique Nationale du Sacré-Coeur** Right **Maison d'Erasme**

TOP 10 Best of the Rest

1 Cantillon

If you visit only one brewery museum, this splendid cobwebby example should be it. *Rue Gheude 56, 1070 BRU (Anderlecht) • Map A4 • 02 521 49 28 • www.cantillon.be • Open 9am–5pm Mon–Fri, 10am–5pm Sat • Closed Sun & public hols • Adm charge*

2 Maison d'Erasme

This charming red-brick house where Dutch humanist Erasmus stayed in 1521 is now a museum. *Rue du Chapitre 31, 1070 BRU (Anderlecht) • Map F2 • 02 521 13 83 • www.erasmushouse.museum • Open 10am–6pm Tue–Sun • Adm charge*

3 Béguinage d'Anderlecht

Tiny *béguinage (see p86)* – now a museum showing how the *béguines* lived. *Rue du Chapelain 8, 1070 BRU • Map F2 • 02 521 13 83 • Open 10am–noon, 2–5pm Tue–Sun • Adm charge*

4 Basilique Nationale du Sacré-Coeur

The largest Art Deco building ever built? Remarkable view from its copper-green dome. *Parvis de la Basilique 1, 1081 BRU (Ganshoren) • Map F2 • 02 425 88 22 • Open Easter–Oct: 9am–5pm; Nov–Easter: 10am–4pm • Free (adm charge for panorama only)*

5 Hôtel Hannon

Spectacular Art Nouveau mansion with a staggering staircase fresco. *Ave de la Jonction 1, 1070 BRU (Saint-Gilles) • Map F2 • 02 538 42 20 • Open 11am–6pm Wed–Fri, 1–6pm Sat & Sun • Adm charge*

6 Muséum des Sciences Naturelles

See complete dinosaur skeletons. *Rue Vautier 29 • Map F5 • www.naturalsciences.be • Open 9:30am–5pm Tue–Fri, 10am–6pm Sat & Sun • Adm charge*

7 Serres Royales de Laeken

Fabulous royal greenhouses. *Ave du Parc Royal (Domaine Royal), 1020 BRU • Map G1 • 02 551 20 20 • Open Apr–May • Adm charge*

8 Musée René Magritte

Magritte's modest abode. *Rue Esseghem 135, 1090 BRU • Map F1 • 02 428 26 26 • www.magrittemuseum.be • Open 10am–6pm Wed–Sun • Adm charge*

9 Maison Autrique

Victor Horta's first project. *Chaussée de Haecht 266, 1030 BRU (Schaerbeek) • Map G2 • www.autrique.be • Open noon–6pm Wed–Sun • Adm charge*

10 Bruparck

Family leisure park. *Bvd du Centenaire 20, 1020 BRU • Map F1 • 02 474 83 83 • www.bruparck.com • Opening hours vary; check in advance • Adm charge*

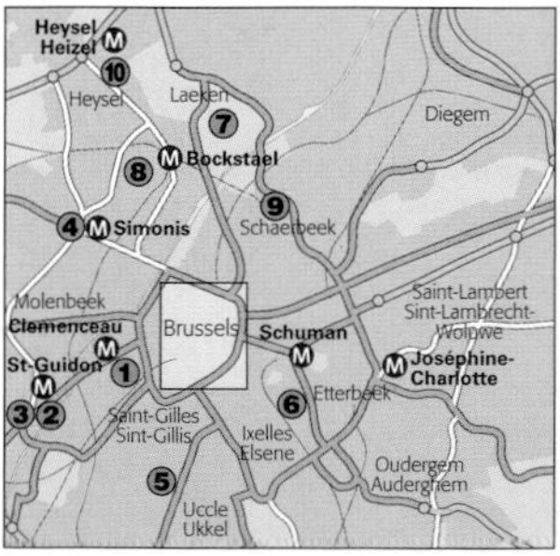

La Quincaillerie

Price Categories

For a three course meal for one with half a bottle of wine (or equivalent meal), taxes and extra charges.	€ under €30
	€€ €30–€40
	€€€ €40–€50
	€€€€ €50–€60
	€€€€€ over €60

TOP 10 Restaurants, Cafés and Bars

1 Bruneau
One of Brussels' finest restaurants. Chef Jean-Pierre Bruneau has two Michelin stars. *Ave Broustin 73–5, 1083 BRU (Ganshoren) • Map F1 • 02 421 70 70 • www.bruneau.be • Closed Tue, Wed • €€€€€*

2 La Quincaillerie
The spectacular interior of this converted hardware store and the exciting menu make up for the gruff service. *Rue du Page 45, 1050 BRU (Ixelles) • Map G2 • 02 533 98 33 • www.quincaillerie.be • Closed Sun L • €€€*

3 Belgo Belge
This lively brasserie is very popular with locals for its classic Belgian dishes at reasonable prices. *Rue de la Paix 20, 1050 BRU (Ixelles) • Map D6 • 02 511 11 21 • €€*

4 Le Chapeau Blanc
A charming brasserie serving excellent mussels and oysters (in season), and steaks. *Rue Wayez 200,1070 BRU (Anderlecht) • Map F2 • 02 520 02 02 • €€€*

5 Rouge Tomate
Mediterranean fare that is ideal for vegetarians. *Ave Louise 190, 1050 BRU (Ixelles) • Map C6 • 02 647 70 44 • Closed Sat L & Sun • €€€€*

6 Balmoral
"Happy Days"-style 1960s diner praised for its burgers and milkshakes. *Place Georges Brugmann 21, 1050 BRU (Ixelles) • Map G2 • 02 347 08 82 • Closed Mon • €€*

7 La Canne en Ville
A delightful restaurant in a delicately converted butcher's shop. French-based cooking. *Rue de la Réforme 22, 1050 BRU (Ixelles) • Map G2 • 02 347 29 26 • Closed Sat L, Sun & weekends Jul & Aug • €€€€*

8 Café Belga (Flagey building)
Trendy café that draws a young arty crowd. Small wonder, given its setting in the extraordinary 1930s Art Deco Flagey radio building. Also a thriving music venue. *Place Eugène Flagey • Map G2 • 02 640 35 08 • www.cafebelga.be*

9 Chez Moeder Lambic
A welcoming pub devoted to beer, with 450 kinds on offer. *Rue de Savoie 68, 1060 BRU (Saint-Gilles) • Map G2 • 02 539 14 19*

10 L'Ultime Atome
Trendy brasserie where locals come to drink artisan beers and French red wine. *Rue St Boniface 14, 1050 BRU (Ixelles) • Map D5 • 02 511 13 67 • Closed Sun • €€*

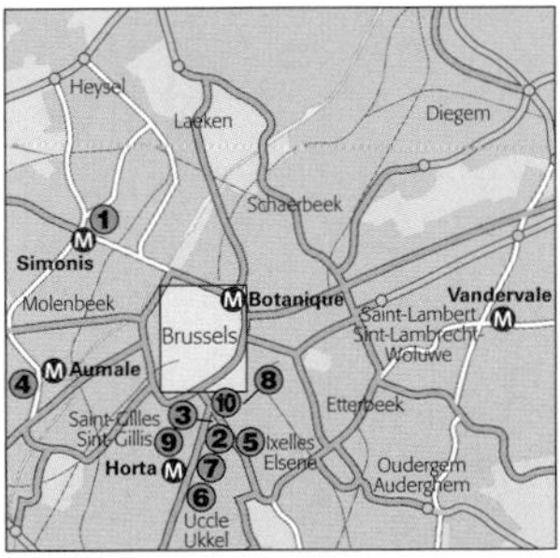

Left ***Portrait of a Bruges Family* by Jacob van Oost (Groeningemuseum)** Right **Sint-Janshospitaal**

Bruges

IN THE MIDDLE AGES, BRUGES *was one of Europe's most prosperous cities. Its wealth derived from trade which brought silks, furs, Asian carpets, wine, fruits, and even exotic pets to its busy network of canals. Then in about 1500 Bruges fell from grace and slumbered for four centuries. It remained a pocket-sized medieval city, its poverty alleviated by almshouses, pious institutions, and a cottage industry supplying Europe's thirst for lace. In the late 19th century, antiquarians recognized Bruges as a historic gem, and began a campaign of preservation and restoration. The city has been a popular tourist destination ever since. In addition to its host of hotels, restaurants and bars, Bruges has internationally famous collections of art. It is also a wonderfully walkable city, with surprising views on every corner.*

Belfort

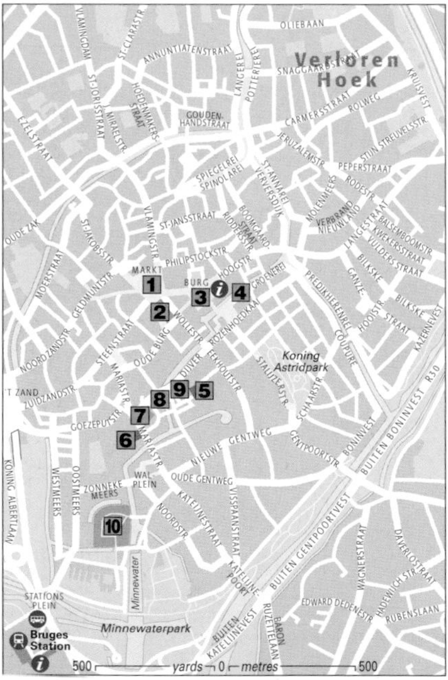

Top 10 Sights

1. Markt
2. Belfort
3. Burg
4. Steenhouwersdijk and Groenerei
5. Groeningemuseum
6. Sint-Janshospitaal and the Memlingmuseum
7. Onze-Lieve-Vrouwekerk
8. Gruuthusemuseum
9. Arentshuis
10. Begijnhof

1 Markt

The central marketplace of Bruges still retains much of its original outline and is the focal point of the city. It is the site of a market on Wednesday mornings, and a Christmas market (with an ice rink) in December. Discover what 15th-century Bruges was like at the Markt's absorbing, multi-sensory Historium museum. *Map K4 • Museum open 10am–6pm Mon–Wed & Fri–Sun, 10am–9pm Thu • www.historium.be • Adm charge*

2 Belfort

For a breathtaking view over Bruges' medieval streets, climb the 366 steps to the top of the Belfort (belfry). The set of bells at the top include the 47 carillon bells that are rung by a mechanism installed in 1748. But they can also be played manually from a keyboard on the floor below by the town's *beiaardier* (carillon player) – Bruges' highest paid official, as the joke goes. *Markt 7 • Map K4 • Open 9:30am–5pm daily (last entry 4:15pm) • Adm charge*

3 Burg

This intimate and fetching square – a glittering confection of historic architecture, sculpture and gilding – was the focal point of old Bruges *(see pp22–3)*.

Groenerei

4 Steenhouwersdijk and Groenerei

Just south of the Burg is one of the prettiest stretches of canal, where calm waters reflect the medieval bridges and skyline. Here, the Steenhouwersdijk (stonemason's embankment) becomes the Groenerei (green canal) and is flanked by a picturesque almshouse called De Pelikaan, dated 1714 and named after the symbol of Christian charity, the pelican. *Map L4*

5 Groeningemuseum

Not only is this one of the great north European collections, with star roles played by the late medieval masters of Flemish painting, such as Jan van Eyck and Hans Memling; it is also refreshingly small *(see pp24–5)*.

Markt

6 Sint-Janshospitaal and the Memlingmuseum

Hans Memling (1435–94) was one of the leading artists of Burgundian Flanders, and the St John's Hospital ranked among his most important patrons. Visitors are advised to use the excellent audioguides available with the entry ticket. The old medieval hospital wards display a fascinating miscellany of treasures, paintings and historic medical equipment; there is also a 15th-century pharmacy. The exhibition culminates in the chapel, which contains the hospital's priceless collection of Memling paintings *(see pp24–5).*

Onze-Lieve-Vrouwekerk

7 Onze-Lieve-Vrouwekerk

The towering spire of the Church of Our Lady is another key landmark of Bruges' skyline. It's a strange architectural mish-mash: the exterior is a good example of the rather austere style known as Scheldt Gothic, and was built over two centuries from 1220 onward. The interior is essentially Gothic, with Baroque flourishes to its statues and extravagant pulpit (1743). This is a rather surprising setting for one of the great treasures of northern Europe: Michelangelo's *Madonna and Child* (1504–5) – a Carrara marble statue that came here by virtue of Bruges' close links to Renaissance Italy, and the only sculpture by Michelangelo to leave Italy during his lifetime. The church's museum includes the beautiful gilt-brass tombs of Charles the Bold (1433–77), Duke of Burgundy, and his daughter Mary (1457–82). *Mariastraat • Map K5 • Open 9:30am–5pm Mon–Sat, 1:30pm–5pm Sun • Adm charge for museum (church free)*

Béguinages

A feature of the Low Countries, these communities were founded in the 13th century as sanctuaries for the many women *(béguines)* left single or widowed by the Crusades. Although deeply pious, a *béguinage* or *begijnhof* was not a convent: the *béguines* could leave to marry. Surviving *béguinages* are still used for social housing, with their modest charms intact.

8 Gruuthusemuseum

If it is hard to picture quite how life was led during Bruges' past, this museum will do much to fill in the gaps. It presents a rich collection of everyday artifacts from the homes of the merchant classes, from kitchen-ware to musical instruments, furniture, textiles and weapons. The 15th-century building was once the palace of the Lords of Gruuthuse, who became wealthy through a tax on beer flavourings *(gruut)*; as a mark of their status, the house has a gallery over-looking the choir of the Onze-Lieve-Vrouwekerk next door. The house was restored in the 19th century to exhibit the pieces that founded this collection. *Dijver 17 • Map K4 • Open 9:30am–5pm Tue–Sun • Adm charge (with Archaeological Museum,* see p41*)*

9 Arentshuis

Frank Brangwyn (1867–1956) was a gifted painter, born in Bruges, the son of William Curtis Brangwyn, one of a group of British artists and architects involved in restoring the city to its Gothic glory. Frank Brangwyn donated an impressive collection of his work to the city. It is now exhibited on the upper floor of the late-18th-century Arentshuis. The ground floor is used for temporary exhibitions. *Dijver 16 • Map K4 • Open 9:30am–5pm Tue–Sun • Admission charge*

10 Begijnhof

This beautiful enclave, home to a community of *béguines (see box)* from 1245 until 1928, expresses something essential about the soul of Bruges. Around the tree-shaded park are the 17th- and 18th-century white-washed homes of the *béguines*. You can visit the grounds, the *béguinage* church and one of the houses *(Begijnhuisje)*. *Wijngaardstraat • Map K5 • Grounds open 6:30am–6:30pm daily. Begijnhuisje open 10am–noon & 2:30–5pm Mon–Sat, 2:30–5pm Sun • Adm charge to Begijnhuisje (grounds free)*

Begijnhof

A Day In Bruges

Morning

A day of wandering. Begin in the **Burg** *(see pp22–3)* and head south across Blinde Ezelstraat. Linger beside the canals on **Steenhouwersdijk** and **Groenerei** *(see p85)*; walk through Huidenvettersplein to the **Dijver** for the prettiest views of the city. Now make your way past **Onze-Lieve-Vrouwekerk** *(see opposite)* to **Mariastraat** and **Katelijnestraat**, where you could stop for a divine hot chocolate at **De Proeverie** *(see p91)*. Take Wijngaardstraat to the **Begijnhof** *(see left)*, loop around the **Minnewater** *(see p88)*, and head back along Katelijnestraat. Note the almshouses that pop up in several places on this street (for instance at Nos 87–101 and 79–83).

For lunch, try the **Vismarkt** area – Wijnbar Est, for example *(see p91)*.

Afternoon

Now you are going to pass through the city's medieval trading centre. From the **Markt** *(see p85)* walk up Vlamingstraat. At **Beursplein**, there was a cluster of national "lodges" – headquarters of foreign traders – such as the **Genoese Lodge** (No 33). One of Bruge's more unusual attractions is also on Vlamingstraat. The **Frietmuseum** *(see p88)* is dedicated to the humble *frites*. Then walk up Langerei to follow the canal that eventually leads to **Damme** *(see p63)*, where goods were transferred from ships to canal barges. Head back down Sint-Jakobstraat, taking a detour to **'t Brugs Beertje** *(see p91)*, with its famed collection of beers.

Left **Minnewater** Right **Huisbrouwerij De Halve Maan**

TOP 10 Best of the Rest

1 Sint-Salvatorskathedraal

It was at St Saviour's that the Order of the Golden Fleece met in 1478. *Steenstraat • Map K4 • Open 2–5:30pm Mon, 9am–noon & 2–6pm Tue–Fri, 9am–noon & 2–3:30pm Sat, 9–10am & 2–5pm Sun • Free*

2 Huisbrouwerij De Halve Maan

Follow the beer-making process at this brewery, in operation since 1856. *Walplein 26 • Map K5 • 050 44 42 22 • www.halvemaan.be • Tours Apr–Oct: 11am–4pm daily (to 5pm Sat); Nov–Mar: 11am & 3pm Mon–Fri, 11am–5pm Sat, 11am–4pm Sun • Adm charge*

3 Godshuis De Vos

The almshouses *(godshuizen)* of Bruges are easily identified by their humble whitewashed walls, inscribed with names and dates. This delightful example dates from 1643. *Noordstraat 2–8 • Map K5*

4 Minnewater

Romantic, willow-lined lake formed by a sluice gate on the River Reie – a hectic port in medieval times. *Map K6*

5 Diamantmuseum

The history of diamonds explained. *Katelijnestraat 43 • Map K5 • 050 34 20 56 • www.diamondmuseum.be • Open 10:30am–5:30pm daily • Closed 2nd & 3rd weeks Jan • Adm charge*

6 Sint-Walburgakerk

This handsome Jesuit church, built in 1619–43, is a Baroque symphony in black and white marble, with a supreme wooden pulpit. *Sint-Maartensplein • Map L3 • Easter–Sep: 8–10pm daily • Free*

7 Frietmuseum

A museum dedicated to the Belgian's adored *frites*. *Vlamingstraat 33 • Map K3 • 050 34 01 50 • www.frietmuseum.be • Open 10am–5pm daily • Adm charge*

8 Choco-Story

A 15th-century *taverne* now devoted to educating visitors about the history and production of chocolate. *Wijnzakstraat 2 • Map L3 • 050 61 22 37 • www.choco-story.be • Open 10am–5pm daily • Adm charge*

9 Sint-Gilliskerk

The pretty parish church of St Giles is unusual for the barrel vault over its nave. Burial place of Hans Memling. *Map L2 • Open May–Sep: 10am–noon & 2–5pm Mon–Sat, 11am–noon & 2–5pm Sun • Free*

10 Sint-Jakobskerk

The church of St James is Bruges' richest parish church, containing notable paintings and tombs. *Map K3 • Open Jul–Aug only: 2–5:30pm Mon–Fri & Sun, 2–4pm Sat • Free*

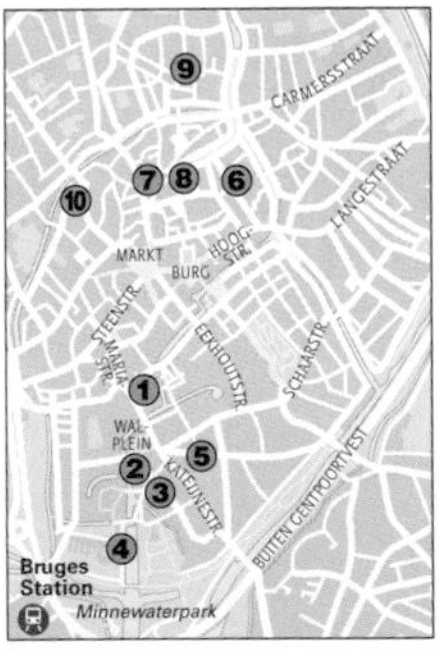

Peaceful Minnewater is a popular spot for walkers and picnickers

Left **Kantcentrum** Right **Kruispoort**

TOP 10 Eastern Bruges: Sint-Anna

1 Onze-Lieve Vrouw ter Potterie
This charming little museum combines treasures, oddities and an elaborate Baroque chapel. *Potterierei 79 • Map L1 • Open 9:30am–12:30pm, 1:30–5pm Tue–Sun • Adm charge*

2 Duinenbrug
Bruges' canals were spanned by little drawbridges to allow boats to pass. This one is a reconstruction from 1976. *Map L2*

3 Museum voor Volkskunde
Occupying eight 17th-century almshouses in the east of the city, Bruges' folk museum presents a fascinating collection of historic artifacts. *Balstraat 43 • Map L3 • Open 9:30am–5pm Tue–Sun • Adm charge*

4 Sint-Annakerk
Elegantly refurbished after destruction by the iconoclasts, this pretty church is a tranquil place of worship enlivened by Baroque flourishes. *Map L3 • Open Apr-Sep: 10am–noon & 2–5pm Mon–Sat, 2–5pm Sun • Free*

5 Guido Gezelle-museum
Rustic home of one of the best-loved poets in Dutch (and Flemish), the priest Guido Gezelle (1830–99). *Rolweg 64 • Map M2 • Open 9:30am–12:30pm & 1:30–5pm Tue–Sun • Adm charge*

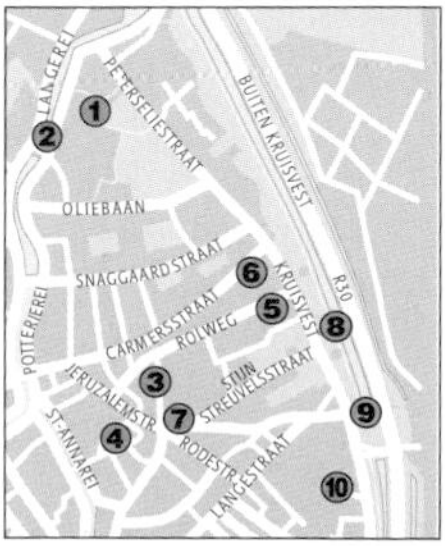

6 Schuttersgilde Sint-Sebastiaan
This historic archers' guildhouse still functions as an archery club. *Carmersstraat 174 • Map M2 • 050 33 16 26 • Open Apr–Sep: 10am–noon Tue–Thu, 2–5pm Sat; Oct–Mar: 2–5pm Tue–Thu & Sat • Adm charge*

7 Jeruzalemkerk and the Kantcentrum
A real curiosity – a 15th-century private chapel inspired by pilgrimages to Jerusalem. Next door is the Kantcentrum (Lace Centre), which has a shop. *Peperstraat 3a • Map L3 • Open 10am–5pm Mon–Sat. Closed public hols • Adm charge*

8 Windmills on the Kruisvest
Two of the city's four remaining flour windmills – Sint-Janshuismolen and Koeleweimolen – are open to the public. *Map M2 • Open 9:30am–12:30pm & 1:30–5pm Tue–Sun (Sint-Janshuismolen: May–Aug; Koeleweimolen: Jul & Aug) • Adm charge*

9 Kruispoort
One of only four surviving gates of the city walls. *Map M3*

10 Muur der Doodgeschotenen
A bullet-marked wall commemorates a dozen men executed by the German army during World War I. *Map M3*

Left **The Bottle Shop** Right **Saturday morning market, 't Zand**

TOP 10 Shopping

1 Steenstraat and Zuidzandstraat

The main shopping area links the Markt to 't Zand. Clothes, shoes, chocolates – they're all here. *Map K4*

2 Zilverpand

This warren of arcades between Zuidzandstraat and Noordzandstraat consists mainly of clothes boutiques. *Map K4*

3 Sukerbuyc

There are chocolate shops at every turn in Bruges, but "Sugarbelly" is family-run and the cocoa treats are handmade on site. *Katelijnestraat 5 • Map K5*

4 The Bottle Shop

Bruges has two well-known breweries, De Gouden Boom and De Halve Maan. The Bottle Shop sells their beers, plus the full Belgian range. *Wollestraat 13 • Map K4*

5 Apostolientje

There are still some lace-makers in Bruges, though not the 10,000 there were in 1840. A number of lace shops line Breidelstraat between the Markt and the Burg, but this one is the most authentic. *Balstraat 11 • Map L3*

6 2be

This shop in a converted 15th-century mayor's house stocks beers, chocolate and biscuits. The bar upstairs offers good canal views. *Wollestraat 53 • Map L4*

7 Huis Van Loocke

Bruges attracts many artists, and several excellent shops cater for their needs. This one has been run by the same family for three generations. *Ezelstraat 17 • Map L4 • Closed Sun, Mon L*

8 Pollentier-Maréchal

This fine shop sells old prints, many of them of Bruges. *Sint-Salvatorskerkhof 8 • Map K5 • Closed Sun & Mon*

9 Markets

General markets are in the Markt (Wednesday mornings) and on 't Zand (Saturday mornings). There is also a small but magical Christmas market in the Markt. Flea markets are held weekend afternoons on Dijver and at the Vismarkt. *Map J4, K4, L4*

10 Supermarkets

The major supermarkets (such as Louis Delhaize) are in the suburbs, but a few small ones, such as Profi, lie within the city. *Langestraat 55 • Map L4*

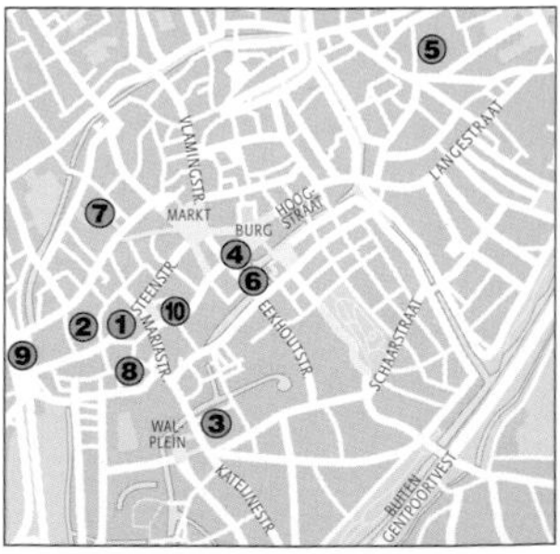

Left **De Proeverie** Right **Café Vlissinghe**

TOP 10 Cafés, Tearooms and Bars

1 De Garre
A well-known old *staminee* (pub), hidden down an alleyway. Famous for its 11 per cent beer. *De Garre 1 (off Breidelstraat) • Map K4*

2 Café Vlissinghe
Said to be the oldest Bruges tavern, founded 1515. Van Dyck apparently met local painters here. Serves light lunches. There's a boules court outside. *Blekerstraat 2 • Map L3 • Closed Mon & Tue*

3 De Proeverie
This delightful little coffee shop belongs to the chocolatier opposite: hot chocolate is a speciality. *Katelijnestraat 6 • Map K5 • Closed Mon*

4 Bittersweet
Friendly, family-run café praised for its hot chocolate, waffles and tasty lunch menu. *Sint-Amandsstraat 27 • Map K4 • 050 34 87 69*

5 Wijnbar Est
A tiny, red brick house that backs onto the canal with live jazz every Sunday from 8pm. Serves snacks and an excellent selection of wines. *Braambergstraat 7 • Map L4 • 050 33 38 39 • Closed Tue*

6 De Versteende Nacht
Bruges has limited night life, but this jazz café has a welcoming crowd and good basic cooking. *Langestraat 11 • Map L3 • Open evenings only, Mon–Sat*

7 Joey's Café
A fun café-bar with low-lit tables, comfy chairs and friendly staff. Hosts occasional free concerts. *Zilversteeg 14 (off Zuidzandstraat) 16a • Map K4 • 050 34 12 64 • Closed Sun*

8 't Brugs Beertje
One of the great beer pubs, serving no fewer than 300 types of beer, including local brews Brugse Zot and Straffe Hendrik. *Kemelstraat 5 • Map K4 • Closed Wed*

9 The Vintage
This lively bar decorated with vintage paraphernalia is located just around the corner from the tourist information centre. *Westmeers 13 • Map K5 • 050 34 30 63*

10 De Republiek
A large, time-worn bar where the young staff create a vibrant atmosphere. Good for cocktails too. DJs play sets on Friday and Saturday nights. *Sint-Jakobstraat 35 • Map K3 • 050 34 02 29*

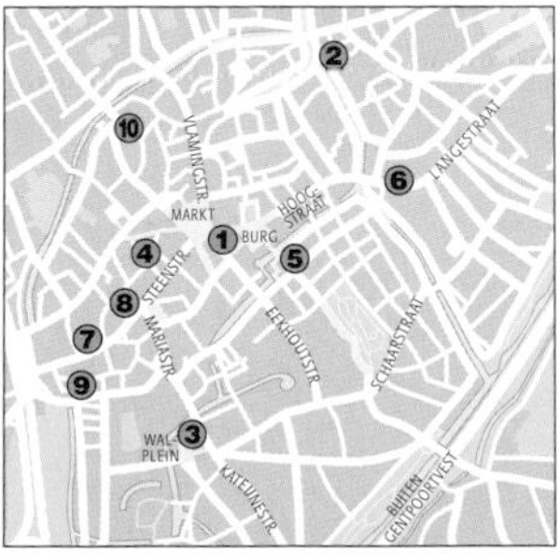

Left **De Karmeliet** Right **Den Dyver**

TOP 10 Restaurants

1 De Karmeliet

With three Michelin stars, this is one of Belgium's top restaurants. Exquisite. *Langestraat 19 • Map L3 • 050 33 82 59 • Closed Sun, Mon, Jan & late Jun–mid-Jul • €€€€€*

2 Patrick Devos

A restaurant cherished for chef Patrick Devos' creative touch, in an elegant *belle époque* house. *Zilverstraat 41 • Map K4 • 050 33 55 66 • Closed Wed D, Sat L, Sun • €€€€€*

3 Den Gouden Harynck

Housed in an attractive 17th-century house, this is one of Bruges' finest restaurants. Book ahead. *Groeninge 25 • Map L5 • 050 33 76 37 • Closed Sun, Mon & last two weeks Jul • €€€€€*

4 Den Gouden Karpel

A fine fish restaurant beside the Vismarkt (fish market), with an excellent fish-shop/*traiteur* next door. *Huidenvettersplein 4 • Map L4 • 050 33 34 94 • Closed Mon • €€€€*

5 Bistro de Schaar

This snug restaurant is renowned for its steaks grilled over an open fire and homemade desserts. *Hooistraat 2 • Map M4 • 050 33 59 79 • Closed Wed • €€€*

6 Rock Fort

Pared-down modern interior in an old family house. The two young owners bring flair to the contemporary cuisine. *Langestraat 15 • Map L3 • 050 33 41 13 • Closed Sat & Sun • €€€€*

7 Den Dyver

Exciting, inventive two-, three- or four-course menus where each course is designed to match an accompanying beer. *Dijver 5 • Map L4 • 050 33 60 69 • Closed Tue & Wed • €€€€*

8 Den Amand

A small restaurant serving inventive dishes of worldwide inspiration. *Sint-Amandsstraat 4 • Map K4 • 050 34 01 22 • Closed Sun, Wed D • €€€*

9 Marieke van Brugghe

Dine beneath a replica panel from the Sistine Chapel at this cosy bistro that serves good beer-soaked stews. *Mariastraat 17 • Map K4 • 050 34 33 66 • Closed Thu • €€€*

10 De Stoepa

Head to this Mediterranean-style café to enjoy lunch from a good menu of tapas, salads and soups. There's a leafy, summer terrace. *Oostmeers 124 • Map K5 • 050 33 04 54 • Closed Mon • €*

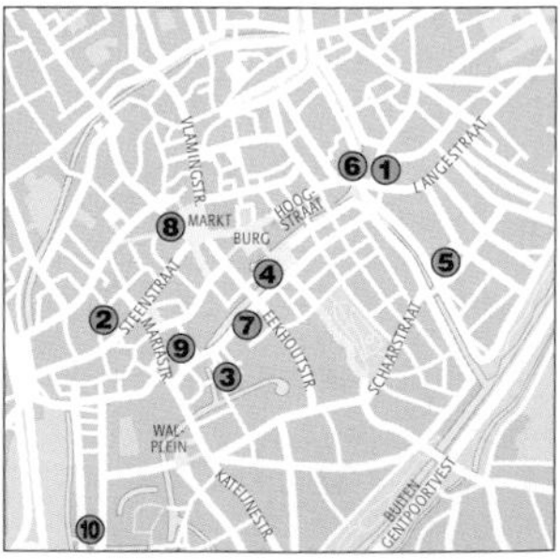

Bruges is an excellent place to try out classic Belgian dishes **See p57**

Het Dagelijks Brood

Price Categories

For a three course meal for one with half a bottle of wine (or equivalent meal), taxes and extra charges.

€	under €30
€€	€30–€40
€€€	€40–€50
€€€€	€50–€60
€€€€€	over €60

Top 10 Lunch Stops, Brasseries, Bistros

1 Bistro de Pompe
This very popular bistro serves an excellent value weekday lunch menu. On offer are hearty meals and salads. *Kleine Sint-Amandstraat 2 • Map K4 • 050 61 66 18 • Closed Sun D, Mon • €€€*

2 Het Dagelijks Brood
Or "Le Pain Quotidien" in French. Part of an esteemed chain providing wholesome sandwiches on crusty bread, plus pâtisserie and other snacks. *Philipstockstraat 21 • Map K4 • €*

3 Pas Partout
The chefs at Pas Partout are unemployed individuals learning a new trade. They serve the cheapest steak *frites* in town! *Jeruzalemstraat 1 • Map L3 • 050 33 62 43 • Closed Sun • €*

4 De Belegde Boterham
A "minimalist" lunch boutique" specialising in open sandwiches along with soups, salads and cakes. *Kleine Sint-Amandsstraat 5 • Map K4 • 050 34 91 31 • Closed Sun • €*

5 Salade Folle
A deservedly popular lunch spot and tearoom serving light, mainly vegetarian dishes, including soups, salads, and home-made cakes. *Walplein 13–14 • Map K5 • 050 34 94 43 • Closed Tue D, Wed • €*

6 Lotus
This lovely vegetarian café is housed in the former residence of prolific painter Jacob van Oost. *Wapenmakersstraat 5 • Map L4 • Open 11:30am–2pm Mon–Sat • €€*

7 Bean Around the World
An American-style coffee house with good coffee, milkshakes and cakes, including home-made apple pie. Free Wi-Fi. *Gonthof 5 • Map L3 • Closed Tue & Wed morning • €*

8 In't Nieuw Museum
In this old family-run tavern, the meat is cooked on an open fire (evenings) in a 17th-century fireplace. Traditional and very friendly. *Hooistraat 42 • Map M4 • 050 33 12 80 • Closed Wed • €€*

9 Gran Kaffee de Passage
A wonderful dark-wood dining room lit mainly by candles is the setting for this restaurant. Gran Kaffee is highly respected for its solid, good-value Belgian dishes. *Dweersstraat 26 • Map K4 • 050 34 02 32 • €*

10 Brasserie Medard
Legendary among locals for its strong sangria and €4 bowls of home-made spaghetti. *Sint-Amandsstraat 18 • Map K4 • 050 34 86 84 • Closed Thu • €*

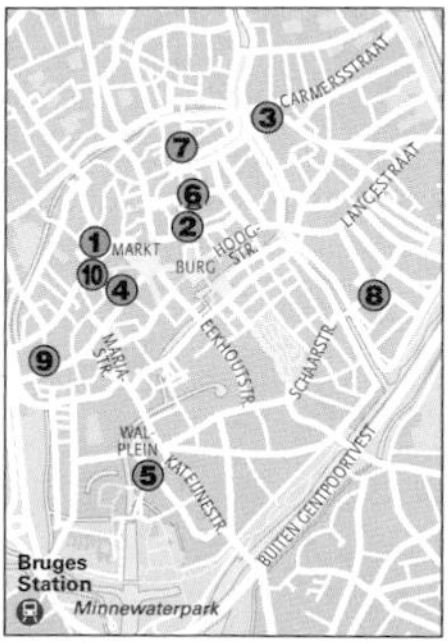

Left ***Adoration of the Mystic Lamb* (central panel) by Hubrecht and Jan van Eyck** Right **Graslei**

Ghent

GHENT HAS MUCH IN COMMON WITH BRUGES. *It is a city with a rich legacy of medieval buildings and art treasures inherited from its days as a semi-autonomous and prosperous trading centre. The tranquil waters of its canals mirror the step-gables of its old guildhouses and the tall spires of its three famous towers. Unlike Bruges, however, historically prosperous Ghent took on a new lease of life as Belgium's first industrial city in the early 19th century. It is also home to a large and famous university. These factors have endowed the city with a scale, bustle, and youthful verve that have shaped its character. Ghent has an elegant grandeur, symbolized by its cathedral, theatres and opera house; but it also has an intimacy, and the web of its medieval street plan – including Europe's largest pedestrianized zone – makes this a perfect city for wandering. It is no surprise, perhaps, that Ghent is the preferred city of many regular visitors to Flanders.*

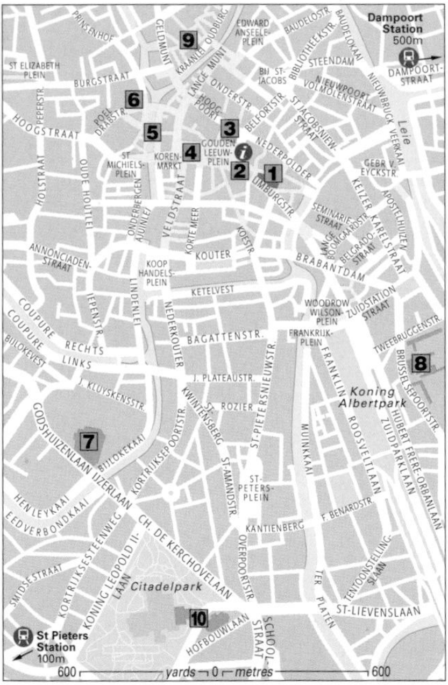

Sint-Niklaaskerk

Top 10 Sights

1. Sint-Baafskathedraal
2. Belfort
3. Stadhuis
4. Sint-Niklaaskerk
5. Graslei and Korenlei
6. Design Museum Gent
7. STAM
8. Klein Begijnhof
9. Het Huis van Alijn
10. Museum voor Schone Kunsten and SMAK

For Ghent tourist information visit www.gent.be

1 Sint-Baafskathedraal

St Bavo was a local 7th-century saint. The cathedral named after him dates back to the 10th century, but most of it is Gothic, built over three centuries after 1290. Outstanding are the grandiose Baroque-Rococo pulpit of oak and marble (1741–5) and the church's greatest treasure the multi-panelled, 15th-century altarpiece, *The Adoration of the Mystic Lamb* by Hubrecht and Jan van Eyck *(see pp26–7).* *Sint-Baafsplein • Map Q2 • 09 269 20 45 • Open Apr–Oct: 8:30am–6pm Mon–Sat, 9:30am–6pm Sun; Nov–Mar: 8:30am–5pm Mon–Sat, 9:30am–5pm Sun (only open to non-worshippers after 1pm Sun) • Adm charge (*Mystic Lamb *only)*

2 Belfort

Ghent's belfry is a prominent landmark, rising 91 m (299 ft) to the gilded dragon on the tip of its spire. It was built in 1380–81 and served for centuries as look-out tower, clock and alarm. It houses a 54-bell carillon, which is used for regular concerts. There is a lift to the top. *Sint-Baafsplein • Map Q2 • 09 233 39 54 • Open 10am–6pm daily • Adm charge*

Throne room, Stadhuis

Sint-Baafskathedraal

3 Stadhuis

Standing on the main square is the impressive town hall. It has a series of regal council chambers, still in use today – some dating back to the 15th century, others refurbished during restoration after 1870. *Botermarkt 1 • Map Q2 • Open May–Sep: 2:30–4:30pm daily, book and depart from Sint-Veerleplein tourist office (Sat & Sun, includes tour of historical centre and St Bavo's) • Adm charge*

4 Sint-Niklaaskerk

St Nicholas, Bishop of Myra, was patron saint of merchants, and this was the merchants' church. Built in the 13th to 15th centuries, it is Belgium's best example of the austere style called Scheldt Gothic. *Cataloniëstraat • Map Q2 • Open 2–5pm Mon, 10am–5pm Tue–Sun • Free*

5 Graslei and Korenlei

The Graslei and Korenlei are departure points for canal trips. The two quays are lined with the step-gabled guildhouses of merchants and tradesmen that date back to the 12th century. Sint Michielsbrug, the bridge at the southern end, offers the best views of the city. *Map P2*

6 Design Museum Gent

This museum is a must for anyone with the slightest interest in furniture, furnishings and interior decoration. Housed in a grand 18th-century mansion, plus an uncompromisingly modern extension, it provides a tour through changing European styles from the 17th century to the present. The Art Nouveau collection is particularly rewarding, with work by Horta, Hankar and Lalique. *Jan Breydelstraat 5 • Map P1 • 09 267 99 99 • www.designmuseumgent.be • Open 10am–6pm Tue–Sun • Adm charge*

Design Museum

7 STAM

The Abdij de Bijloke, an old rambling Cistercian convent and hospital, provides a superb setting for STAM, Ghent's City Museum. Covering the history of the city from prehistoric times to the present day, STAM incorporates the vast range of items of the former Bijloke Museum, including medieval tombs, freemasons' regalia and models of warships. The convent dates from medieval times, but most of the buildings are 17th-century. *Godshuizenlaan 2 • Map P4 • 09 269 14 00 • www.stamgent.be • Open 10am–6pm Tue–Sun • Adm charge*

Ghent and Charles V

Charles V (1500–58), Holy Roman Emperor, King of Spain, master of much of Europe and the New World, was born in Ghent, and his baptism in Sint-Baafskathedraal was celebrated with a huge feast. But the city's love affair with its famous son went sour when it found itself endlessly squeezed for taxes. A revolt in 1540, and the execution by hanging of its ringleaders, gave rise to the people of Ghent being called the *stroppendragers* ("noose bearers") – a proud symbol of their defiant and independent spirit.

8 Klein Begijnhof

There are three *béguinages* *(see box, p86)* in Ghent, but this is by far the prettiest. With step-gabled, whitewashed houses set around a little park and Baroque church, it is a classic of its kind – a fact recognized by its status as a UNESCO World Heritage Site. It was founded as a community of single women in about 1235, and has been continuously occupied, although the residents are no longer *béguines*. Most of the present houses date from the 17th century. *Lange Violettestraat 205 • Map R4 • Open 6:30am–10pm daily • Free*

9 Het Huis van Alijn

Just north of the centre of Ghent is a quaint and folksy quarter called the Patershol, a warren of little medieval streets and alleys. This is the backdrop for one of the best folk museums in Belgium. A huge and fascinating collection of artifacts – toys, games, shoes and crockery, as well as complete shops and craftsmen's workshops – are laid out within almshouses set around a grassy courtyard. These almshouses

were founded in 1363 as a children's hospital – not as an act of pure philanthropy but as penance for the murder of two members of the Alijn family.
Kraanlei 65 • Map Q1 • 09 269 23 50 • Open 11am–5pm Tue–Sat, 10am–5pm Sun • Adm charge

10 Museum voor Schone Kunsten (MSK) and SMAK

Ghent's two leading museums of art are a short tram or bus ride south of the city centre. The MSK (Fine Arts Museum) covers painting and sculpture from the Middle Ages up to the early 20th century and has a world-class and eclectic collection of works by a number of important artists, such as Hieronymus Bosch, Rogier van der Weyden and Hugo van der Goes. Opposite the MSK, and in more ways than one, is the Stedelijk Museum voor Acktuele Kunst (SMAK), which is Ghent's superb modern art gallery. Its challenging permanent collection – with pieces by Magritte and Broodthaers – and regularly changing temporary exhibitions have placed SMAK at the forefront of modern art galleries in Europe. *Citadelpark • Map Q6 • MSK: 09 240 07 00. www.mskgent.be; SMAK: 09 221 07 03. www.smak.be • Open 10am–6pm Tue–Sun • Adm charges*

Museum voor Schone Kunsten

A Day in Ghent

Morning

SMAK and the **Museum voor Schone Kunsten** *(see left)* make a good double act – a stimulating mixture of fine art and pure provocation, from world-class artists. Get these under your belt early in the day (note that they're closed on Mon). Trams 1 and 10 run from the central Korenmarkt to Charles de Kerchovelaan, from where you can walk through or beside the **Citadelpark** to the museums. These will absorb the greater part of the morning; you can break for refreshments at SMAK's café. For lunch, head back into the city centre. The Korenmarkt is equidistant from two enticing and contrasting lunch options: **The House of Eliott** *(see p99)*, and the medieval **Groot Vleeshuis** *(see p98)*.

Afternoon

Now go to **Sint-Baafskathedraal** to see the **Mystic Lamb** *(see pp26–7)*. Then you can go up the **Belfort** *(see p95)* to get a view over the city. Now it's back to the Korenmarkt, stopping off at the **Sint-Niklaaskerk** *(see p95)*, then over to the **Graslei** and **Korenlei** *(see p95)* to drink in the views. This could be the time to take a canal trip. From the Korenlei, walk along Jan Breydelstraat and take the first right into Rekeligestraat to reach the **Gravensteen** (Castle of the Counts). Then cross the Zuivelbrug and take Meerseniersstraat to the **Vrijdagmarkt** (Friday Market) for beer at **Dulle Griet** *(see p98)* and chips with mayonnaise at **Frituur Jozef** *(see p99)*.

Left **'t Dreupelkot** Right **Groot Vleeshuis**

Top 10 Shops, Cafés and Bars

1 Mageleinstraat and Koestraat
Ghent claims to have the largest pedestrianized zone of any city in Europe, making shopping all the more agreeable. Most chain stores are in Veldstraat and Lange Munt, but there's more charm around the quieter Mageleinstraat and Koestraat. *Map Q2*

2 Post Plaza
The palatial Neo-Gothic former post office has been cleverly turned into a modern mall of high-profile boutiques. *Korenmarkt 16 • Map Q2*

3 Tierenteijn-Verlent
In situ since 1790, this delicatessen is famous for its home-made mustard pumped up from the cellars into a wooden barrel. *Groetenmarkt 3 • Map Q1 • Closed Sun*

4 Dulle Griet
One of the celebrated "beer academies" of Belgium, with 250 beers on offer. Note the basket in which you must deposit a shoe as security when drinking Kwak, a beer served in its own unique glass. *Vrijdagmarkt 50 • Map Q1*

5 Het Spijker
Cosy candle-lit bar in the cellar of a 13th-century leprosy shelter with a large, popular terrace. *Pensmarkt 3-5 • Map P2*

6 't Dreupelkot
A folksy waterfront bar which serves only *jenever*, a form of gin, variously flavoured with fruit, vanilla, even chocolate. *Groentenmarkt 12 • Map Q1*

7 Groot Vleeshuis
This centre for East Flemish food – part restaurant, part delicatessen – is sensationally located in a medieval butchers' hall. *Groentenmarkt 7 • Map Q1 • 09 223 23 24 • Closed Mon • €*

8 Brooderie
The smell of freshly baked bread wafts around this rustic-style eatery serving sandwiches and light vegetarian fare. *Jan Breydelstraat 8 • Map P1 • Closed Mon • €*

9 Hot Club de Gand
This hidden jewel at the end of a narrow alley, opposite the Butchers' Hall, is tricky to find, but the live jazz most evenings makes the search worthwhile. *Groentenmarkt 15B • Map Q1 • Closed Mon*

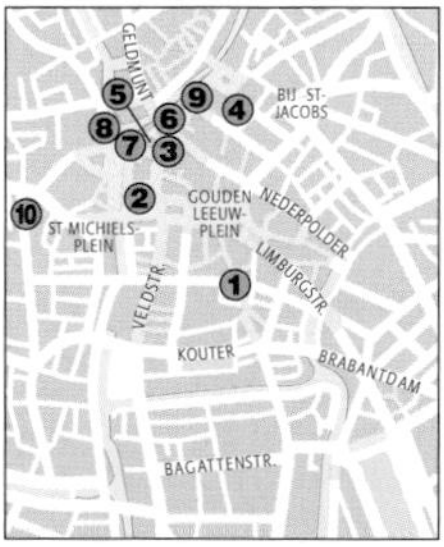

10 Café Labath
A popular locals café serving excellent coffee and hot chocolate, as well as delicous breakfasts, soups and sandwiches. Friendly, relaxed service. *Oude Houtlei 1 • Map P2 • Closed Sun • €*

The House of Eliott

Price Categories

For a three course meal for one with half a bottle of wine (or equivalent meal), taxes and extra charges

€	under €30
€€	€30–€40
€€€	€40–€50
€€€€	€50–€60
€€€€€	over €60

TOP 10 Restaurants

1 Belga Queen
The historic 13th-century building, elegant decor and the quality of the locally sourced food, create a high-end feel at this contemporary restaurant. *Graslei 10 • Map P2 • 09 280 01 00 • €€€€*

2 Bord'eau
Inside the renovated Fish Market, this urbane brasserie's trump card is the stunning views of the Graslei and Korenlei *(see p95)*. *Sint-Veerleplein, Oude Vismijn • Map P1 • €€€€*

3 Brasserie Pakhuis
Run by celebrated restaurant designer Antoine Pinto, Pakhuis is big and very popular – so reserve! *Schuurkenstraat 4 • Map P2 • 09 223 55 55 • Closed Sun • €€€*

4 De Blauwe Zalm
Located in the heart of the medieval Patershol district, this is Ghent's best seafood restaurant. Excellent choice of wines. *Vrouwebroersstraat 2 • Map Q1 • Closed Sun • €€€€€*

5 Korenlei Twee
This 18th-century dockside town house, serves meals using ingredients from the local fish and meat markets. Good value and excellent wine. *Korenlei 2 • Map P2 • 09 224 00 73 • Closed Sun, Mon • €€€€*

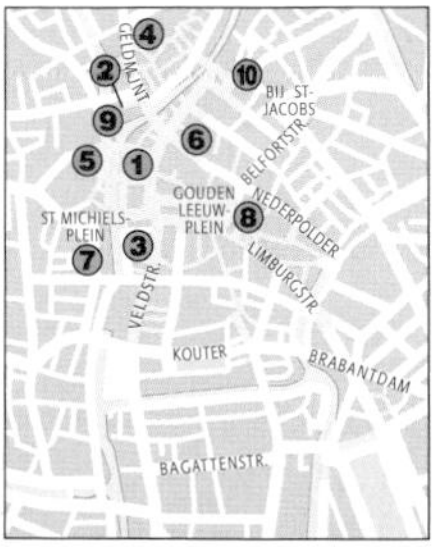

6 Mosquito Coast
Laidback travellers' café adorned with souvenirs from around the world. It offers good vegetarian options, bookshelves of guides and two sunny terraces. *Hoogpoort 28 • Map Q2 • €€*

7 Coeur d'Artichaut
Pared-down elegance in an old mansion, with patio. Light, wholesome, international cuisine prepared to high standards of excellence. *Onderbergen 6 • Map P2 • 09 225 33 18 • Closed Sun, Mon • €€€€*

8 Brasserie De Foyer
This excellent brasserie is dramatically located within the grand 19th-century Koninklijke Nederlandse Schouwburg (theatre), with a balcony overlooking Sint-Baafskathedraal. Crêpes and waffles are served in the afternoons; popular buffet brunch on Sundays. *Sint-Baafsplein 17 • Map Q2 • 09 234 13 54 • Closed Mon, Tue • €€€*

9 The House of Eliott
Joyously eccentric pseudo-Edwardian restaurant overlooking the canal. *Jan Breydelstraat 36 • Map P1 • 09 225 21 28 • Closed Tue, Wed • €€€€*

10 Frituur Jozef
Old-established chip stand serving perfect chips (fries) and all the trimmings. *Vrijdagmarkt • Map Q1*

When in Ghent, you should try the city's classic dish, Waterzooi **See p57**

Left **Koninklijk Museum voor Schone Kunsten** Right **Rubenshuis**

Antwerp

SET ON THE BROAD RIVER SCHELDT, *at the gateway to the North Sea, Antwerp is one of the leading trading cities of northern Europe; and in the early 17th century it was one of the great cultural centres too. The city, though, has had its share of suffering – battered by the religious wars of the 16th century, cut off from the North Sea by treaty with the Netherlands from 1648 to 1795, and bombed in World War II. These historical ups and downs have endowed the city with a keen edge, like its famous diamonds. This dynamic energy is seen today in its hip bars, restaurants and nightclubs.*

TOP 10 Sights

1. Grote Markt
2. Onze-Lieve-Vrouwekathedraal
3. Rubenshuis
4. Koninklijk Museum voor Schone Kunsten (KMSKA)
5. Museum Aan de Stroom (MAS)
6. Museum Plantin-Moretus
7. Vleeshuis
8. Sint-Jacobskerk
9. Rockoxhuis
10. Museum Mayer van den Bergh

Statue of Brabo, Grote Markt

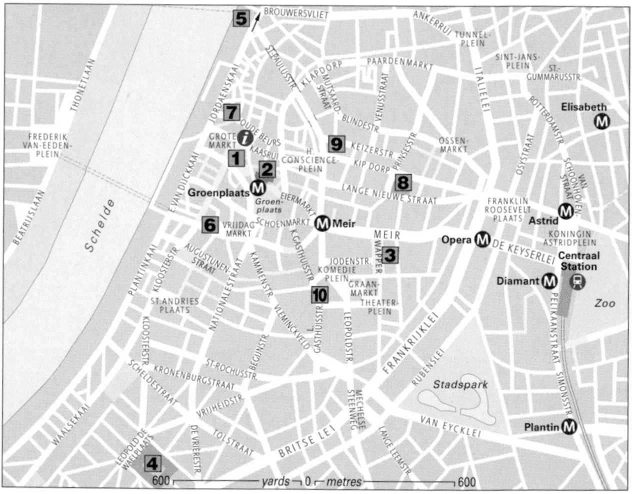

Preceding pages **Selection of Belgian pralines**

Grote Markt

1 Grote Markt

The main square of Antwerp is one of the great gilded arenas of Belgium. The city authorities made a virtue of its unusual "dog-leg" shape and slope by commissioning sculptor Jef Lambeaux (1852–1908) to create an eye catching fountain, placed off-centre, with its water spilling out onto the cobbles. It depicts Brabo, a legendary Roman soldier who freed the port of Antwerp by defeating the giant Antigoon and throwing his severed hand (*hand-werpen*) into the river. The Italian-influenced Stadhuis (town hall) dominates the square. Built in the 1560s, its grand horizontals are offset by the upward curve of the roof-corners. *Map T1 • Stadhuis: guided tours only, book three weeks ahead (ask at tourist office, Grote Markt 13, 03 232 01 03) • Adm charge*

2 Onze-Lieve-Vrouwekathedraal

This huge Gothic cathedral contains several splendid works by Rubens *(see pp28–9)*.

3 Rubenshuis

A rare opportunity not only to visit the house and studio of one of the great stars of European art, but also to see what a 17th-century patrician home looked like *(see pp30–31)*.

4 Koninklijk Museum voor Schone Kunsten (KMSKA)

Antwerp's fine arts museum is second only to Brussels with its full range of paintings, from early Flemish "Primitives" to the Symbolists, but the Neo-Classical building is undergoing an extensive renovation that will last until late 2017. Some works are on display at Mechelen's Schepenhuis and other locations. For more information either telephone or consult the museum's website. *Leopold De Waelplaats • Map S3 • 03 224 95 50 • www.kmska.be*

5 Museum Aan de Stroom (MAS)

It is impossible to miss this towering dockside museum built of red sandstone and perspex. It uses the city's collection of ethnographic and folkloric treasures to dynamically explore mankind and our interaction with the world. *Hanzestedenplaats 1 • Map U1 • 03 338 44 00 • www.mas.be • Open Apr–Oct: 10am–5pm Tue–Fri & 10am–6pm Sat & Sun, Nov–Mar: 10am–5pm Tue–Sun. Closed pub hols • Adm charge (free first Wed of month)*

Museum Aan de Stroom (MAS)

Museum Plantin-Moretus

6 Museum Plantin-Moretus

Christopher Plantin (c.1520–89) was a French bookbinder who, in 1546, came to Antwerp to set up his own printing workshop. It became one of the most influential publishing houses in Europe during the late Renaissance, producing Bibles, maps, scientific books and much else. The museum consists essentially of the printing workshop and home of Plantin and his heirs. It contains a large collection of rare and precious books, and displays of their illustrations. The processes of hot-metal type setting and letterpress printing are also explained. Plantin gave his name to a typeface still widely used today. *Vrijdagmarkt 22 • Map T2 • 03 221 14 50 • www.museumplantinmoretus.be • Open 10am–5pm Tue–Sun. Closed Mon & public hols • Adm charge (free first Wed of month)*

The River Scheldt

Old Antwerp lies on the east bank of the River Scheldt (or Schelde). The river is so broad that the modern suburb on the west bank seems utterly remote (it is linked by tunnels). The Scheldt is deep enough to bring large ships to Antwerp's docks to the north of the city. This easy access to the North Sea has made Antwerp Europe's second largest port.

7 Vleeshuis

With its turrets and towers and Gothic detail, the "Meat House" is one of the most beautiful buildings of Antwerp. Built in 1501–4 as the guildhouse of the butchers and a meat market, it is now used as a museum of music. From street singers to concert hall, the Vleeshuis charts the history of the city through its many forms of musical expression, using historical instruments, including harpsichords made by the famous Ruckers family, manuscripts and a bell foundry. *Vleeshouwersstraat 38 • Map T1 • 03 292 61 00 • www.museumvleeshuis.be • Open 10am–5pm Tue–Sun • Adm charge (free first Wed of month)*

Vleeshuis

8 Sint-Jacobskerk

Of all the churches in Antwerp, the church of St James is noted for having the richest interior – and for being the burial place of Rubens. It was built in late Gothic style in the 15th and 16th centuries by architects who also worked on the cathedral. The church contains work by leading sculptors of the 17th century, such as Lucas Faydherbe, Artus Quellinus and Hendrik Verbruggen, as well as paintings by Rubens, Jordaens and Van Dyck. *Lange Nieuwstraat 73–75 • Map U2 • 03 232 10 32 • Open 1 Apr–31 Oct: 2–5pm daily • Adm charge*

9 Rockoxhuis

Come here for a glimpse of the grace and elegance of 17th-century patrician style. A series of rooms contains a fine collection of furniture, paintings and artifacts. The house is named after its owner, city mayor Nicholas Rockox (1560–1640), a philanthropist and a friend and patron of Rubens. There are paintings and drawings by Rubens, Jordaens and Van Dyck, as well as work by Frans Snyders (1579–1657), who lived next door. *Keizerstraat 10–12 • Map U1 • 03 201 92 50 • www.rockoxhuis.be • Open 10am–5pm Tue–Sun • Adm charge (free on first Wed of the month)*

10 Museum Mayer van den Bergh

Fritz Mayer van den Bergh (1858–91) was an avid collector of art and curios. When he died, his mother created a museum to display his collections – some 5,000 items in all. They include tapestries, furniture, stained glass, paintings and coins. *Lange Gasthuisstraat 19 • Map T2 • 03 338 81 88 • www.mayervandenbergh.be • Open 10am–5pm Tue–Sun • Adm charge (free on first Wed of the month)*

Museum Mayer van den Bergh

A Day in Antwerp

Morning

This day of gentle ambling takes in many of the key sights of Antwerp, as well as some of the best shopping streets. Start off at the **Vleeshuis** and head for the old city centre – the **Grote Markt** *(see p103)* – and the **cathedral** *(see pp28–9)*. Now thread your way to Wijngaardstraat, and the fetching ensemble of the **Sint-Carolus Borromeuskerk** *(see p106)*, before heading on to the **Rockoxhuis** *(see left)* in Keizerstraat. After this, walk south along Katelijnevest to the **Meir**. The tower block to your right, with KBC on its crest, is the **Boerentoren**, the highest building in Europe when constructed in 1932. Head down the Meir to the **Rubenshuis** *(see pp30–31)*; you can lunch here, or if you prefer at the **Grand Café Horta** *(see p108)*.

Afternoon

Now you've done the culture, you can wander the neighbourhood's shopping streets *(see p107)*. **Schuttershofstraat** is a good place to start. It leads to Huidevettersstraat, the Nieuwe Gaanderij Arcade, Korte Gasthuisstraat and Lombardenvest. If you are up for more museums, the excellent **Museum Mayer van den Bergh** *(see left)* and the **Maagdenhuis** *(see p106)* are just to the south. Alternatively, head for Nationalestraat and Dries van Noten's outlet, the beautiful **Het Modepaleis**, *(see p107)*, and then down to **Pier 19** *(see p108)* or **De Vagant** *(see p109)* for some refreshments.

Left **Sint-Carolus Borromeuskerk** Right **Building in Cogels-Osylei**

Top 10 Best of the Rest

1 Red Star Line Museum
Between 1873 and 1934, Red Star ocean liners departed from Antwerp's docks for the United States, taking families to a new life. This museum explores their journey. *Montevideostraat 3 • Map T1 • 03 206 03 50 • www.redstarline.org • Open 10am–5pm Tue–Fri, 10am–6pm Sat & Sun. Closed public hols • Adm charge*

2 Maagdenhuis
A 16th-century girls' orphanage with paintings by Rubens and Jordaens. *Lange Gasthuisstraat 33 • Map T3 • 03 338 26 20 • Open 10am–5pm Mon, Wed–Fri, 1–5pm Sat & Sun • Adm charge*

3 Fotomuseum Provincie Antwerpen (FOMU)
Antwerp's excellent museum of photography and historical artifacts also contains the MUHKA *(see below)* film museum. *Waalsekaai 47 • Map S3 • 03 242 93 00 • www.fotomuseum.be • Open 10am–6pm Tue–Sun • Adm charge*

4 MUHKA
A former warehouse contains the cutting-edge Museum van Hedendaagse Kunst (contemporary art). *Leuvenstraat 32 • Map S3 • 03 260 99 99 • www.muhka.be • Open 11am–6pm Tue–Sun (11am–9pm Thu). Closed public hols • Adm charge*

5 Sint-Pauluskerk
Gothic and Baroque fight it out in this endearing church. *Veemarkt 13 • Map T1 • 03 232 32 67 • Open 1 Apr–31 Oct: 2–5pm daily • Free*

6 Sint-Carolus Borromeuskerk
Celebrated for its Baroque façade and its tragic loss of 39 Rubens paintings. *Hendrik Conscienceplein 6 • Map T1 • 03 231 37 51 • Open 10am–12:30pm, 2–5pm Mon–Sat; for religious services Sun*

7 Centraal Station
Architect Louis Delacenserie created this grand Neo-Classical station in 1905. *Map V2*

8 Cogels-Osylei
In the late 19th century, this area became a showcase for opulent architecture – extraordinary.

9 Maagdenhuis
Quirky museum with some lovely old masters, in an old orphanage. *Lange Gasthuisstraat 33 • Map T3 • 03 223 56 20 • Open 10am–5pm Mon, Wed–Fri, 1–5pm Sat–Sun. Closed public hols • Adm charge*

10 ModeMuseum (MoMu)
A museum of *haute couture*. *Nationalestraat 28 • Map T2 • 03 470 27 70 • www.momu.be • Open 10am–6pm Tue–Sun • Adm charge*

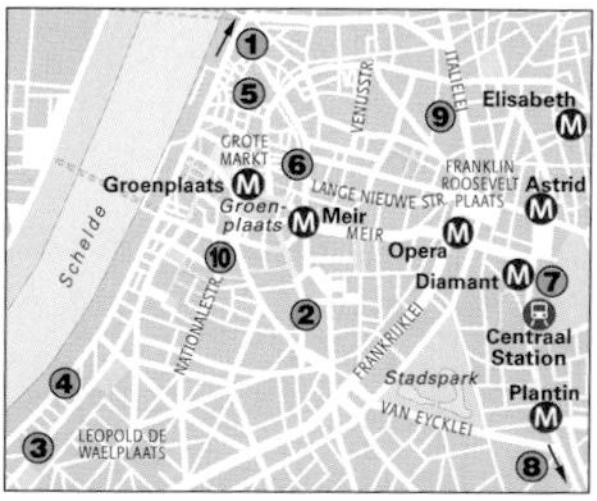

Left **Het Modepaleis** Right **Walter**

TOP 10 Shopping

1 Meir
The main shopping street is a broad pedestrianized avenue, fronted largely by high-street chain stores. *Map U2*

2 Pelikaanstraat
Wall-to-wall diamond and jewellery shops in the Jewish quarter. Fascinating, partly because there's nothing romantic about it – the gems are commodities like any other. *Map V2*

3 Nieuwe Gaanderij Arcade
A good place to snoop for fashion at a slightly lower pitch than the designer boutiques. *Between Huidevettersstraat and Korte Gasthuisstraat • Map T2*

4 Grand Bazar Shopping Center
An elegant modern arcade shares space with the Hilton hotel in the shell of a former department store. *Beddenstraat 2 • Map T2*

5 Nationaalstraat
The heart of Antwerp's *haute-couture* fashion district offers boutiques by many world-class designers but remains accessible to all. *Map T2*

6 Schuttershofstraat
Another street of recherché boutiques and shoe shops, including a branch of the ultimate Belgian accessories manufacturer Delvaux. Smell that leather! *Map U3*

7 Het Modepaleis
This elegant *belle époque* "flat iron" building is the main outlet for one of Antwerp's most fêted fashion designers, Dries van Noten. *Nationalestraat 16 • Map T2*

8 Walter
What looks more like an art gallery than a clothes shop is the showcase for fashion designer Walter van Bierendonck, as well as other select labels. *Sint-Antoniusstraat 12 • Map T2*

9 Ann Demeulemeester
A stone's throw from the MUHKA modern art gallery, Demeulemeester's shop displays the uncompromising edge that has placed her at the forefront of fashion. *Leopold de Waelplaats/ Verlatstraat • Map S3*

10 Diamondland
Special diamonds at lower prices than elsewhere in Europe. *Appelmansstrat 33A • Map V2*

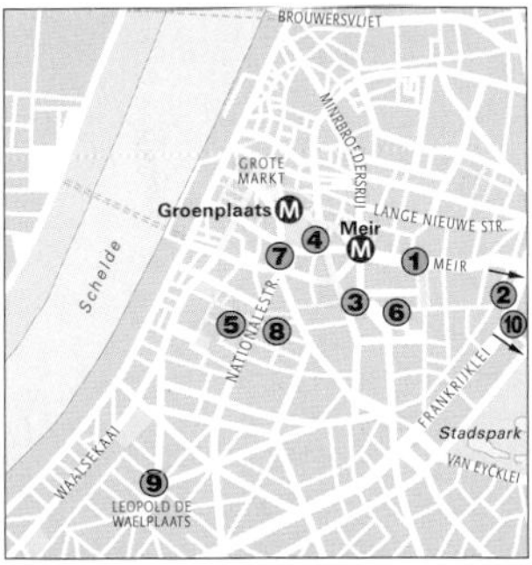

Grand Café Horta

Price Categories

For a three course meal for one with half a bottle of wine (or equivalent meal), taxes and extra charges.

€	under €30
€€	€30-€40
€€€	€40-€50
€€€€	€50-€60
€€€€€	over €60

TOP 10 Cafés and Restaurants

1 Huis de Colvenier

This is one of the most respected restaurants in Antwerp, so you should book in advance. Elegant room and daily changing menu. *Sint-Antoniusstraat 8 • Map T2 • 03 226 65 73 • Closed Sun, Mon • €€€€€*

2 Den Abbattoir

Located next to Park Spoor Noord, this former butchers dishes up ultra-fresh steak and ribs. *Lange Lobroekstraat 65 • Map V1 • 03 271 08 71 • Closed Sun • €€€*

3 Docks Café

Inventive, multi-layered interior by celebrated designer Antoine Pinto. Renowned for its oysters. *Jordaenskaai 7 • Map T1 • 03 226 63 30 • Closed Sun • €€€*

4 Zuiderterras

A landmark building over the River Scheldt, containing an elegant, first-class brasserie. *Ernest van Dijckkaai 37 • Map T2 • 03 234 12 75 • €€€*

5 Pier 19

This warehouse conversion in the old dockland area north of the city houses a lounge club (DJs Thu–Sat), restaurant and lunch spot. *Brouwersvliet 19 • Map T1 • 0478 28 27 83 • Closed Mon, Sun • €€€*

6 Het Vermoeide Model

This brasserie-restaurant creates an intimate mood with medieval beams and live piano music. *Lijnwaadmarkt 2 • Map T2 • 03 233 52 61 • Closed Mon • €€€*

7 Zum

Fun, family-friendly café that serves delicious open sandwiches, quiches, home-made cupcakes and good coffee. *Viaductdam 1 • Map V1 • 03 345 03 36 • Closed Mon • €*

8 Grand Café Horta

A dynamic space created using metal salvaged from Victor Horta's celebrated Art Nouveau Volkshuis in Brussels, demolished in 1965. *Hopland 2 • Map U2 • 03 203 56 60 • €€€*

9 Dôme Sur Mer

Floor-to-ceiling windows and a marble bar make an impressive setting for this hugely popular fish restaurant in the Zurenborg. *Arendstraat 1 • Map V3 • 03 281 74 33 • Closed Sat L • €€€€*

10 Brasserie Appelmans

Brasserie-style dining in a 12th-century building with classic Belgian dishes made from locally sourced ingredients. *Papenstraatje 1 • Map T2 • 03 226 20 22 • €€€*

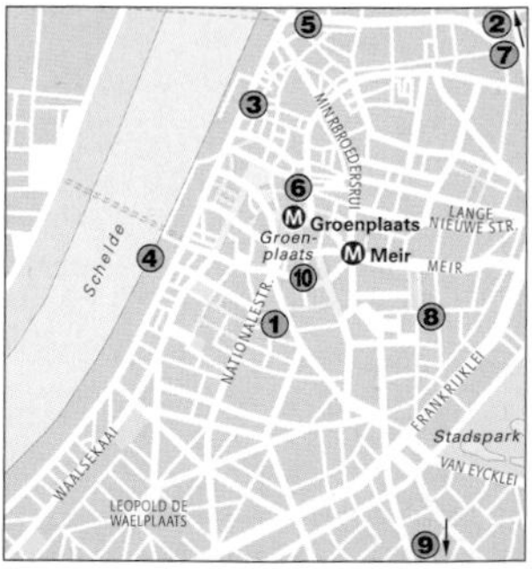

Left **Het Kathedraalcafé** Right **Den Engel**

TOP 10 Bars and Clubs

1 Café d'Anvers
Antwerp's original nightclub is still cool. A great option if you want to listen to a mix of house, soul, disco and funk. *Verversrui 15 • Map T1 • 03 226 38 70*

2 Noxx
Take a taxi to this hip night-club in the northern Het Eilandje district. *Kotterstraat 1 • Map U1 • Open Thu–Sat*

3 Cafe Local
A glamorous complex of themed Latin-American-style areas: Cuban market, high street, ballroom. It holds a salsa night on the first Sunday of the month. *Waalsekaai 25 • Map S3 • 03 238 50 04*

4 D-Club
Lively, predominantly gay, nightclub with popular, free Saturday night parties. Resident and celebrity guest DJs spin the tunes. *Damplein 27 • Map V1 • 0488 49 96 07*

5 Het Kathedraalcafé
Quirky, yet cosy, bar where the walls are packed with gaudy religious icons. A stairway to heaven? *Torfbrug 10 • Map T1*

6 Den Hopper
This jazz bar is very popular with Antwerp's creative set. The drink to ask for is *demi-demi* (half cava; half white wine). *Leopold De Waelstraat 2 • Map S3 • 03 248 49 33*

7 Sips
A chic cocktail bar in the arty dockland area south of the city centre. Cigars are a speciality. *Gillisplaats 8 • 0477 63 91 52*

8 Den Engel
A classic Belgian *bruine kroeg* (brown pub – brown with the patina of age) overlooking the Grote Markt. Try a *bolleke* (chalice-like glass) of De Koninck, Antwerp's cherished own brew. *Grote Markt 3 • Map T1 • 03 233 12 52*

9 De Muze
A friendly pub with live jazz most evenings until 2 or 3am. Exposed beams and brickwork create a cosy ambience. *Melkmarkt 15 • Map T2 • 03 226 01 26*

10 De Vagant
A welcoming traditional café-bar offering some 200 types of *jenever* (gin). You can buy your favourite brand in the Slijterij shop upstairs. *Reynders straat 25 • Map T2 • 03 233 15 38*

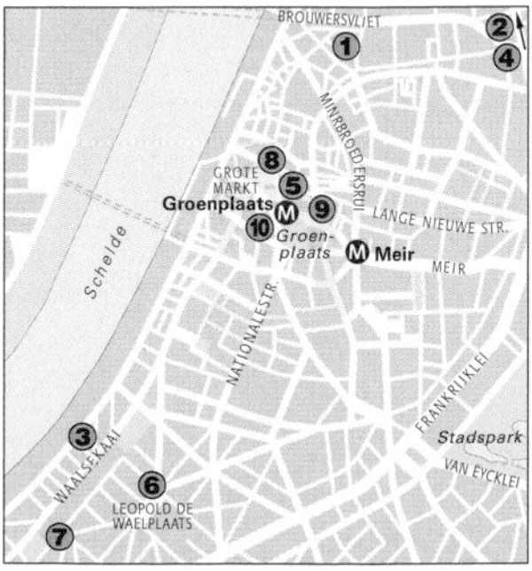

LE GRAIN
DE SABLE

STREETSMART

Left **Accessing information at an internet café** Right **Tourist information sign**

TOP 10 General Information

1 Choose Your City

Brussels, Bruges, Ghent or Antwerp? All share historical interest, art galleries, good hotels and restaurants, and enjoyable shopping. But each is different. Brussels: vibrant capital. Bruges: medieval wonder. Ghent: lively university town. Antwerp: city of trade. Look at the introductions to each city above *(pp66–9, 76–9, 84–7, 94–7 and 102–5)*, and see which one most strikes a chord.

2 Languages

The people of Bruges, Ghent and Antwerp speak Dutch; in Brussels they speak predominantly French or Dutch (some speak the old Bruxellois dialect Marollen). Generally English is fairly widely understood. There is a third official Belgian language, German, spoken in the eastern cantons.

3 National Tourist Offices

There are Belgian tourist offices in most western capitals, operated by the two main tourist authorities: Tourism Flanders–Brussels; and the Belgian Tourist Office–Brussels–Ardennes.

• ***In London**: Tourism Flanders–Brussels, Flanders House, 1a Cavendish Square, London W1G 0LD. Information line: 020 7307 7738. www.visitflanders.co.uk*

• ***In New York**: Belgian Tourist Office, 220 East 42nd Street, Suite 3402, New York NY 10017. 212 758 8130. www.visitbelgium.com*

4 City Tourist Offices

Each city has its own tourist office *(see panel)*, providing detailed local information and assisting with hotel reservations.

5 Internet

National and city tourist offices have useful websites *(see panel)*, providing details of key attractions, events, restaurants and hotels, as well as maps and other links.

6 Weather

Belgian weather is typical for northern Europe: a mix of sunshine and rain, distributed across the four seasons. Average seasonal temperatures range from 1°C (34°F) in winter to 19°C (66°F) in summer.

7 What to Pack

Regarding clothing, assume the worst in weather and you'll be fine. Pack comfortable shoes – you will be walking.

8 Time Difference

Belgium is on Central European Time, one hour ahead of GMT. It observes Daylight Saving Time, so remains one hour ahead of the UK, and six hours ahead of New York, all year round.

9 Electricity and Outlets

Belgium runs on 220 volts AC, using two-pin plugs. The current is fine for most British equipment, but American visitors will need a transformer.

10 Public Holidays

Belgian public holidays are: New Year's Day; Easter Monday; Labour Day (1 May); Ascension Day (6th Thu after Easter); Whit Monday (7th Mon after Easter); Flanders Day (11 July); National (Independence) Day (21 July); Assumption (15 Aug); All Saints' Day (1 Nov); Armistice Day (11 Nov); Christmas Day. Banks and post offices will remain closed; some shops and museums may stay open.

City Tourist Offices

Brussels
Rue Royale 2 • Map D4 • 02 513 89 40 • www.visitbrussels.be

Bruges
Concertgebouw, 'T Zand 35 • Map J5 • 050 44 46 46 • www.brugge.be

Ghent
Sint-Veerleplein, Oude Vismijn • Map P1 • 09 266 56 60 • www.visitgent.be

Antwerp
Grote Markt 13 • Map T1 • 03 232 01 03 • www.visitantwerpen.be

Left **Checking in** Right **Trains at the Gare du Midi, Brussels**

Top 10 Getting There

1 Visas and Entry Requirements
You need a passport to enter Belgium, valid at least three months beyond the end of your stay. Citizens of the EU, the USA, Australia and New Zealand need no visa if staying for less than 90 days. Citizens of other countries should consult their Belgian embassy for information.

2 Customs and Allowances
Most goods can be transported between EU countries, including wines, spirits and tobacco, provided they are for your own personal use, and in quantities that reflect this. For non-EU citizens flying into Belgium, national limits apply.

3 By Air
Most international flights arrive at Zaventem Airport, which is located 14 km (9 miles) north-east of Brussels. There are train links from Brussels to Bruges, Ghent and Antwerp. Some airlines go to Charleroi, 60 km (37 miles) south of the city.

4 Zaventem Airport
You can reach central Brussels from Zaventem Airport by taxi, bus or by train (with around three trains per hour). The bus service ("Airport Line") connects the airport to Brussels' European Quarter.

5 By Train
The central hub of Belgium's rail network is Brussels, which has three main stations: the Gare du Midi (Zuidstation), the Gare Centrale (Centraal Station) and the Gare du Nord (Noordstation). Eurostar trains from London (as well as international TGV and Thalys trains) arrive at the Gare du Midi. There are good train connections with Bruges, Ghent and Antwerp (for onward journeys, *see p114*).

6 Brussels Gare du Midi
The station is connected by bus, tram, metro and taxi to all part of Brussels, but the pictogram signposting is virtually indecipherable; you may need help just to get out of the station! Help is at hand at the tourist office opposite the Eurostar entrance. *Map A5*

7 By Car
To bring a car into Belgium, you must carry a valid EU driving licence, or international driving licence, plus insurance and car registration documents. You must also carry a warning triangle, first-aid kit and fluorescent safety jacket. You will be driving on the right, so adjust the angle of your headlamps if travelling from Britain so that they don't dazzle oncoming drivers.

8 Free Motorways
All the motorways in Belgium are toll-free and most are well maintained. Almost all are well lit at night.

9 Crossing the English Channel
Travellers from Britain can cross the Channel by ferry, or via the Channel Tunnel *(see panel below)*.

10 By Bus
Eurolines runs a regular bus service from London to Brussels, to Antwerp, to Ghent, and to Bruges. There are also bus services that connect the cities of northern Britain to the Hull–Zeebrugge ferry crossing.

Cross Channel Operators in Britain

DFDS Seaways
0871 574 72 35
• www.dfdsseaways.co.uk

P&O Ferries
08716 64 21 21
• www.poferries.com

Eurotunnel
0844 335 35 35
• www.eurotunnel.com

Eurostar
08432 186 186
• www.eurostar.com

Eurolines
08717 818 178
• www.eurolines.co.uk

My Ferry Links
• www.myferrylink.com

Left **Taxis at a taxi rank** Right **Bicycles can be hired throughout Belgium**

TOP 10 Getting Around

1 Distances Between Cities

Belgium is a small place – hardly larger than Wales or New Hampshire – and the four cities are all in the north of the country. Brussels is the farthest south. Antwerp lies 45 km (28 miles) due north of Brussels; Ghent lies to the west and about 50 km (31 miles) from both Brussels and Antwerp; Bruges lies a further 40 km (25 miles) north-west of Ghent.

2 By Train

Belgium's excellent national rail service, called SNCB in French and NMBS in Dutch, is clean, punctual, efficient and reasonably priced. Regular services link all four cities. The website has timetables and prices. *www.belgianrail.be*

3 By Car

Belgian drivers used to have a bad reputation – practical driving tests began only in the 1960s. Today they are no worse than any other European drivers; faults such as driving too close on the motorway *(see p121)* are virtually universal. In the cities, take care of trams, which compete fiercely for road space. See also the note on *priorité de droite* on p121.

4 Parking

There is plenty of parking in and around all the cities. The best plan is to use one of the main public car parks, which are well signposted and not too expensive. City centres get clogged up with traffic at busy times, and car parking there is limited. Especially in Bruges and Ghent, visitors are encouraged to use outlying car parks.

5 Car Rental

All the main car hire agencies operate in Belgium. Usually you get better value if you book a hire car in your home country, linking it with your flight. Note that all the cities are compact; you don't really need a car unless you want to go touring outside the city limits.

6 Taxis

Taxis are available at taxi ranks or can be booked by phone. In Brussels, they can occasionally be hailed on the street – but not usually in the other three cities. They cost quite a lot more than public transport. A 10 per cent tip is customary.

7 City Transport

The main transport systems are bus and tram; Brussels also has a Metro (underground railway or subway), and Antwerp an underground tram system called the Pre-Metro. Use the buttons on board trams and buses to indicate that you wish to get off at the next stop, and to open the doors. Public transport in Brussels is operated by STIB (or MIVB); in the other cities the operator is De Lijn. *www.stib.be; www.delijn.be*

8 Buying Tickets

Tickets for public transport cover buses, trams and Metro. Single tickets, a card valid for 10 journeys, or a one-day pass can be bought at ticket booths or stations. Single tickets for buses and trams are also available from the driver. At the start of a journey, you have to validate the ticket in the orange machine on board a bus or tram, or on entering a Metro station; it is then valid for a single journey of up to an hour, including any changes you need to make.

9 Cycling

Belgians are keen cyclists and traffic is usually respectful. You can hire bikes and equipment in all the cities. The city tourist offices *(see p112)* will provide details of hire companies.

10 On Foot

This is probably the best way of all to get around. In all the cities, most of the things you will want to see are close to the centre, and within easy walking distance of one another. Take a pair of sturdy waterproof shoes.

Left **Cobbled streets in historic towns can make access difficult** Right **Disabled access sign**

TOP 10 Tips for Disabled Travellers

1 Before You Leave

Historic cities such as Brussels, Bruges, Antwerp and Ghent have developed over centuries with scant attention paid to disabled travellers' needs. Although attitudes are changing, adapting the physical environment to meet their needs will take a long time. The tourist authorities have collated information to help disabled people, but there are still large gaps. It is therefore important to do your research before you leave home.

2 Organizations

Among bodies in the UK providing advice and practical help to disabled travellers are Tripscope, Youreable.com and RADAR (Royal Association for Disability and Rehabilitation). Those in the USA include Mobility International and SATH (Society for Accessible Travel and Hospitality). *www.youreable.com • RADAR: 020 7250 3222. www.radar.org.uk • Mobility International: (541) 343 1284. www.miusa.org • SATH: (212) 447 7284. www.sath.org*

3 Information

City tourist offices hold information on, for example, wheelchair-accessible toilets and facilities for disabled people in hotel rooms, but this is not published in collated form on their websites, so telephone or email the offices *(see p112)*. You can also try Access Info, a branch of the Flemish Tourist Board, and VFG, a Flemish organization providing advice for disabled people. *www.accessinfo.be • www.vfg.be*

4 Holiday Companies

Some UK tour operators specialize in travel for disabled people and their companions. Tourism for All has a Benelux guide. Accessible Travel and Leisure (ATL) offers city breaks in Brussels and Bruges. *Tourism for All: 0845 124 9971. www.tourismforall.org.uk • ATL: 01452 729 739. www.accessibletravel.co.uk*

5 Local Attitudes

The Belgians are very sympathetic to the needs of disabled travellers. If you need their help, they will usually be quick to give it. This compensates to some extent for the lack of ramps, adapted bathrooms, wide doors and other aids.

6 Steps and Cobbles

Many key sites are in historic areas where access is hard for disabled people. Some have been adapted, but others elude practical conversion. Bruges, especially, will never be able totally to adapt its winding staircases, narrow pavements and cobbled streets.

7 Museums and Galleries

Most larger museums have adequate facilities for disabled people, including wide entrances, ramps, lifts and adapted toilets. Staff are usually helpful; if in doubt about accessibility, telephone before you visit.

8 Public Transport

The bus, tram and Metro systems, and train stations are generally poorly adapted to use by disabled travellers – although some newer trams have wheelchair access. Tourist offices can offer advice about alternatives, including special taxi services. Belgian Railways has advice pages on its website. *www.belgianrail.be*

9 Accommodation

Many modern or renovated hotels have one or more rooms with special facilities for disabled and wheelchair-bound people. These are indicated in tourist office brochures and on the hotels' websites.

10 Restaurants

Although restaurants are under pressure to improve their provision, the number of those with full disabled access and facilities remains small. A wheelchair symbol in a tourist brochure may be open to a variety of interpretations when it comes to accessibility.

Left **Canal boat trip** Right **Horse and carriage**

Top 10 Specialist and Sightseeing Tours

1 Packaged Tours

Tour operators who arrange both transport and accommodation may offer significant advantages in cost. A reliable tour company will offer a good choice of hotels and courier back-up on the ground. When looking for specialist tours, it's best to do some research on the internet.

2 Art and Cultural Tours

Belgium's rich art history – from Jan van Eyck to the Surrealists – is on display in all four cities. Some specialist tour groups are accompanied by lecturers. Cox & Kings organize a tour of Bruges and Ghent focussing on Flemish art and architecture, while the "Flemish Painting" tour offered by Martin Randall Travel covers all four cities.

3 Gastronomy and Beer

Check with tourist offices *(see p112)* for details of gastronomic tours. Some tour operators offer trips centred on Belgian beer or chocolate. American company InTrend Travel has a seven-day "chocolate-lovers' paradise tour" of Bruges, Brussels and Antwerp. The itinerary includes chocolate-making demonstrations at various chocolate producers and chocolate-themed meals. BeerTrips.com run escorted tours and short breaks.

4 Battlefield Tours

Ypres *(see p63)* is the focus of many tours incorporating World War I battlefields, trenches, cemeteries and memorials. Specialist battlefield tour operators organize complete trips, including transport and accommodation. Guided day trips or specialized tours are also offered to Waterloo *(see p62)*.

5 City Guided Tours

Local tourist offices *(see p112)* organize regular guided walks around all four city centres.

6 City Bus Tours

Buses, some with multilingual headphones, tour all the main sights – a very effective way of getting a quick overview of a city.

7 Canal Boats

Despite being inland, both Bruges and Ghent were once thriving ports by virtue of their canals – or rather, their canalized rivers. Today, canal trips are popular ways to tour the cities. Tour boats leave from various points in the city centre. You can also take trips on the more industrialized canal of Brussels.

8 Horse-drawn Carriages

It is possible to travel through Bruges, Ghent and Antwerp city centres by horse and carriage, or horse-drawn tram. This is particularly popular in Bruges, a city well suited to such transport. Although it is expensive and short-lived, the experience is unforgettable.

9 Private Guides

Tourist offices can arrange for a private guide to show you around a city, or take you to see a particular aspect of a city. Most of these guides belong to one of the professional guide associations.

10 Themed Walks and Tours

Guided walks and car tours have a wide range of themes, including Jewish history, industrial architecture, and beer. ARAU in Brussels offers many tours focusing on Art Nouveau.

Specialist Tour Operators

ARAU
www.arau.org

BeerTrips.com
www.beertrips.com

Cox & Kings
www.coxandkings.co.uk

Flanders Battlefield Tour
www.ypres-fbt.com

Intrend Travel
www.intrend.com

Martin Randall Travel
www.martinrandall.com

Left **Friterie** Right **Delicatessens: a source of first-class picnic food**

Top 10 Ways to Save Money

1 Off-season Travel

During school holidays and around the major feast days, flights and Channel crossings are more expensive, but hotel prices fluctuate wildly according to the ebb and flow of business travel, which means that hotel prices may actually be cheaper during the high season *(see also p118, Weekend Rates)*. There are times when cheaper off-season travel costs and hotel bargains coincide.

2 Passes for Public Transport

A multi-journey public transport pass can save money. This is particularly relevant in Brussels, where you may wish to travel to the museums and sights of Outer Brussels, beyond normal walking distance. A "10-journey" ticket covers 10 individual journeys on different days by bus, tram and Metro. A one-day pass allows you to take as many journeys as you like on a single day.

3 Rail Discounts

You get a 50 per cent discount on return and round-trip rail fares if you travel between 7pm on Friday and Sunday night. Children under 12 can travel for free. The Go-Pass e-ticket allows under-26s to go anywhere in Belgium for €6 one way. Senior citizens aged over 65 also pay a flat-rate price of €6 for a return journey anywhere after 9am on weekdays, except on published restricted days.

Belgian Railways: www.belgianrail.be

4 Park and Walk

Car parking is most expensive in city centres, and much cheaper – free, even – on the outskirts. In Bruges, for instance, parking at the station in the south-west of the city is less than half the price of parking in the centre. Parking at metered bays is also available, but only for short stays.

5 Museum Discounts

Ask at the tourist office about schemes that allow you to visit several museums for a single price.

6 Free Museums

Some museums, such as the Musée Royal de l'Armée et d'Histoire *(see p77)*, are free. Others have free days. The Musée Royaux des Beaux-Arts *(see pp12–15)* and the Musée Royaux d'Art et d'Histoire *(see p77)* are free on the afternoon of the first Wednesday of the month. The Rubenshuis *(see pp30–31)* is free on the last Wednesday of every month.

7 Lunch-time Bargains

Many restaurants offer set menus at a fixed price for two or three courses. You can also eat well in most cafés and bars, which offer simple dishes like soup, salad, pasta or steak and chips, or traditional snacks such as *croque monsieur* (ham and cheese on toast).

8 Friteries

Belgian chips are a meal in themselves, but a good chip stall *(friterie/frietkot)* has a wide range of accompaniments, including sausages, meat balls, fish cakes, and even a stew of beef cooked in beer. Together, they make a delicious, very cheap and very Belgian meal.

9 Picnics

Delicatessens, bread shops and pâtisseries offer delicious prepared food – sandwiches, flans, tarts, tubs of salad. Pick up a first-class meal and head for a park.

10 Youth Hostels

Youth hostels offer by far the cheapest accommodation in Belgium – under €20 for a double room. Most offer a mixture of two-, three-, four and six-bedroom dormitories with shared washing facilities, although there's an increasing trend for upmarket hostels that offer en-suites. Hostels also have lively bars, kitchens for preparing your own meals, and internet facilities – all good for meeting other travellers.

If you can make lunch your main meal, you can find bargains in the set menus of top restaurants.

Left **Bruges has many hotels of charm and character** Right **Bed-and-breakfast accomodation**

TOP 10 Accommodation Tips

1 Internet Information

There is a great deal of information about hotels, facilities and prices on the internet. Most hotels have their own websites, with links for enquiries and bookings.

2 How to Book

You can book by fax, internet or telephone (almost all reception staff speak English). Many hotels require security for a booking, such as a credit card number. The city tourist office *(see p112)* can also help you to find a room.

3 The Star System

The official star system for rating hotels is based more on facilities than on things that really make a difference, such as decor, tranquillity and quality of service. Two-star hotels may actually be more rewarding and agreeable than five-star ones. Le Dixseptième in Brussels *(see p125)* must rank among the most delightful hotels in the world, but it only has four stars, not five.

4 Weekend Rates

Many hotels offer weekend rates (Fri–Sun and public holidays), which are far cheaper that the standard "rack rate". In Brussels, the cheap rate may cover July and August, and through much of December to mid-January. Many hotels also offer discounted rates if you stay several nights. Prices quoted may not include city tax, which is usually €2 extra.

5 High and Low Seasons

Hotels prices reflect the predicted ebb and flow of business and holiday trade. Summer is busy in Bruges, but less so in Brussels, Antwerp or the university city of Ghent.

6 Hotels of Charm

For small hotels that are very comfortable and full of character, Bruges and Ghent are way ahead of the other cities. In Antwerp, such hotels are scarce; an exception is Matelote *(p131)*. Brussels has more to offer *(see p125)*.

7 Business Hotels

The hotel industry in Belgium is run with professionalism at all levels. In the business sector, pricing is highly competitive; the more you pay, the more you get – in terms of the facilities, at least.

8 Breakfast

Check whether breakfast is included in the price – it can cost €15 a head or more if you pay separately. A hotel breakfast usually consists of a buffet, with cereals, croissants, cold meats and cheese, fruit, yogurts and juices, and sometimes bacon and eggs.

9 Bed and Breakfast

Private citizens in the cities are, in increasing numbers, opening their homes for bed-and-breakfast accommodation. Some of these are delightful historic houses, right in the centre. They are good value for money – around €55–€95 for a double room, per night – and the best tend to be booked up months in advance. You can find many of the properties on the Internet. Tourist offices can also provide listings and contacts *(and see panel below)*.

10 Camping and Caravanning

A cheap option, at under €20 per family per night, is to stay at one of Belgium's efficiently run camping and caravanning sites. Needless to say, they are not near the city centres. Tourist offices will have details.

Bed-and-Breakfast

Bed & Breakfast Antwerpen
• *www.gastenkamers antwerpen.be*

Bed & Brussels
• *www.bnb-brussels.be*

Corporation of Bruges B&B
• *www.brugge-bedandbreakfast.com*

Guild of Guesthouses in Ghent
• *www.bedand breakfast-gent.be*

Left **Fixed-price menus** Right **Restaurant bills usually include service**

TOP 10 Eating and Drinking Tips

1 The Language of Food

French was traditionally the language of menus, especially in the smarter restaurants. Today, in the Flemish cities, Dutch may lead, followed by English, perhaps with no French at all. But it is rare to find a restaurant with no one to explain the dishes in exquisite detail – in whatever language suits you best.

2 Follow the Locals

The Belgians love eating out, and they want good food at good prices. If a restaurant is not up to scratch, they simply don't go there. If their favourite restaurant goes through a bad patch, they desert it. So choose the restaurants that are full of locals.

3 Make a Reservation

Good restaurants are busy every day of the week. If you set your heart on going to a particular one, be sure to make a booking – easy enough to do over the telephone. If you change your mind, be sure to cancel the reservation.

4 Fixed-price Menus

Special two- or three-course menus offered at a fixed price *(dagschotel* or *dagmenu)*, which often change on a daily basis, can be extremely good value. It's not simply a question of price; the chefs may have found ingredients at the market that took their fancy, and will be concentrating extra creative talents on them.

5 Vegetarians

Belgium is essentially a carnivorous and fish-loving nation, but most restaurants provide vegetarian options. There are also some dedicated vegetarian restaurants in all the cities, where chefs apply characteristic Belgian flare to their dishes. Tourist offices have listings.

6 Bloody, Rare and Well-done

Belgians like their beef fairly rare. If you ask for a medium-rare steak *("saignant")*, it is likely to be more rare than medium. The beef's quality usually justifies light cooking, but if you want your meat well done *("bien cuit")*, insist on it. Lamb is also served rare; if you don't like it that way, ask for it to be well done when you order.

7 Raw Meat, Raw Oysters

In certain dishes, beef is served raw. This applies to *Steak Américain (see p56)* and the widely adopted Italian dish *carpaccio*. Fish is served raw in the Japanese-influenced fusion dishes, and in salmon or tuna *carpaccio*. Oysters are likewise eaten raw.

8 Bills, Tax and Tipping

Value-added tax (TVA/BTW) at 21 per cent and a service charge of 16 per cent can add a lot to a restaurant bill, but both are usually included in the prices quoted in the menu. If you are not sure, don't be afraid to ask. If service is not included, you can add 10 per cent; if it is, you can add a small cash tip, but this is optional.

9 Eating with Children

Eating out is often a family event in Belgium; lunch can last half the afternoon. Children get used to this from an early age and may develop surprisingly sophisticated tastes. As a result, children are almost always welcomed in restaurants, and restaurateurs will go out of their way to satisfy their eating and drinking preferences. Children are also allowed into most cafés and bars.

10 Beer Strength

Belgian beers are generally somewhat stronger than their equivalents in Britain and the USA, and range from about 5% to 12% alcohol by volume. Since beers are served in fairly small quantities, the effect can be deceptive – until you stand up. It may need a bit of practice to get the measure of this.

For more on Belgian food See pp56–7

Left **Selection of beers** Right **Supermarket counter**

TOP 10 Shopping Tips

1 Tax Refunds
Visitors from outside the EU can reclaim most sales tax (TVA/BWT) on purchases above a minimum value of €125 from any one shop. Look for shops with the Tax-free Shopping sign. With sales tax at 21 per cent, this means a large saving on items of high value. You must obtain a "Tax-free Shopping Cheque" from the shop, and you can claim your refund at the Tax-free offices at Zavantem Airport. Visit www.global-blue.com or www.brusselsairport.be for more information.

2 Customs Allowances
EU residents face few limits on taking goods out of Belgium, but some restrictions apply to meat products, plants and, of course, weapons and narcotics. Alcohol and tobacco must be for personal use only; UK guidelines for maximum quantities are 10 litres of spirits, 800 cigarettes, 90 litres of wine, and 110 litres of beer. Non-EU visitors returning home are subject to more restrictive limits on alcohol and tobacco.

3 Opening Hours
As a general rule, shops are open from 10am to 6pm; small shops such as bakeries and newsagents may open earlier. Some shops close for lunch but stay open later in the evening. On Sundays, larger shops and supermarkets close, but pâtisseries, chocolate shops, delicatessens and tourist shops are likely to remain open. Some shops stay open late on one night of the week, but none of the cites has a general late-night-shopping day.

4 Supermarkets
Many goods worth taking home – Trappist beers, Stella Artois lager, Côte d'Or chocolates – are found in supermarkets. The larger markets, such as those of the Delhaize chain, tend to be in the suburbs, but they also have mini stores in town.

5 Shopping Malls
All the cities have covered shopping malls *(see pp 71, 90, 98 and 107)*, which are home to up-market boutiques and clothing chains.

6 Buying Chocolates
One of the great things about good-quality Belgian filled chocolates, or pralines, is that they contain fresh cream – but as a result they also have a limited shelf-life. If you refrigerate them, however, they should be fine for about three weeks.

7 Beer and Wine
Belgian beer is remarkably good value, given its quality. There are specialist beer shops, but most of the better-known beers can be bought in ordinary food shops and supermarkets. The Belgians tend to drink French wine, and shop prices for wine are similar to French prices.

8 Genuine Lace
Genuine, hand-made lace is expensive. To ensure you are getting the real thing, insist on a certificate of authenticity *(see p54)*.

9 Fashion
The city centres are packed with all sorts of clothes shops. Many items are imported, but the prices may still seem good value. Belgium is also famous for its home-grown designers. Antwerp is the fashion design centre and has a throng of shops that reflect this *(see p107)*, but the clothes of the top designers can be found in outlets elsewhere. There are also several respected Belgian labels (such as Olivier Strelli and Rue Blanche), with shops in most cities.

10 Books in English
All the cities have plenty of bookshops; the best offer many books in English, including novels and guidebooks. Brussels has several specialist English-language bookshops, including a branch of Waterstone's. *Boulevard Adolphe Max 71–75 • Map C1*

Left **Most museums and galleries are closed on Monday** Right **Pedestrian crossing**

TOP 10 Things to Avoid

1 The Fast Lane

Do not be tempted to imitate Belgian drivers in motorway fast lanes. They tend to drive nose-to-tail at top speed, as if the concept of "stopping distance" had gone out of fashion.

2 Pedestrian Crossings

Well, you shouldn't *avoid* pedestrian crossings – but treat them with care. The law obliging drivers to stop for pedestrians waiting to cross the road was introduced only in 1996. Previously, drivers would tend to ignore pedestrian crossings unless someone actually walked in front of them. Some drivers still seem to follow this rule; others stop punctiliously.

3 Priorité de Droite

In the past, traffic coming in from the right had priority, known as *priorité de droite*. Road markings now indicate that priority belongs to traffic on the main road, and that traffic joining a main road must give way. But vestiges of *priorité de droite* survive, notably in suburban streets in Brussels, so keep an eye out for road markings and traffic approaching from your right.

4 Drinking and Driving

Drinking-and-driving is illegal. One alcoholic drink, and you'll probably be just within the limit; two drinks and you may be over the limit – and, if stopped by police, liable to hefty penalties.

5 Driving into Bruges

Bruges does all it can to encourage you to park in one of the big car parks on the periphery of the city. The best solution is to go along with this, and walk the 1 km (half a mile) from the car parks to the city centre. However, it is possible to drive to your hotel and, indeed, to park close to the city centre, especially outside of the summer high season.

6 Mosquitoes

The canals of Bruges (and, to a lesser extent, those of Ghent) have always been a breeding ground for mosquitoes. This can be a nuisance in summer, so don't forget your insect repellent. If you fear that mosquitoes will bother you, choose an air-conditioned hotel, where you can keep the windows shut.

7 Getting Caught Short

Where there are public toilets in the cities, they are usually well run by caretakers, who ask for a contribution of about €0.30 for use of the facilities. Alternatively, use bar or café toilets – but, if you do so, behave like a customer and buy a drink or a coffee.

8 High Season in Bruges

Bruges is very busy in summer. Tour coaches arrive in droves, and release their throngs at car parks in the south-west of the city to pour into the streets leading to the centre. One way of dealing with this is to stay several days, so you can see the city in its more tranquil moments. Another is to explore the quieter areas – just about anywhere but the south-west. Still another is to come at a different time of year (but Bruges can be busy year-round).

9 Visiting Museums on Mondays

Monday is the day of rest for just about all the major museums and galleries – so it's a good day for walking, shopping, visiting churches, or whatever else takes your fancy.

10 Tourist Restaurants

You can spot them a mile off: plastic-coated menus printed in at least four languages; waiters who solicit your custom at the door; an entirely foreign clientèle; and restaurant terraces that occupy the most desirable locations in the city centre. Don't be tempted. The food in tourist restaurants is generally mediocre and poor value. Hunt a little further afield, or ask a local where to eat. The effort will be repaid.

It's almost impossible to eat badly in Belgium, but eating well may take a little research.

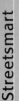

Left **International papers on a news stand** Right **Post office**

Top 10 Banking & Communications

1 Changing Money

Belgium's currency is the euro. Notes of other currencies and travellers' cheques can be changed or cashed at a bank or at one of the specialist exchange bureaus. To check whether or not you are getting a good deal, look at both the rate of exchange offered and the commission charged.

2 Banking Hours

Banks are generally open Mon–Fri 9am–noon and 2–4pm, but some larger branches do not close for lunch. Some banks also open on Saturday mornings. The exchange bureaus have longer opening hours, and may be open through the weekend.

3 ATMs

Bank and credit cards can be used to draw cash from an ATM (Automatic Teller Machine). Before travelling, check with the bank or card issuer that your card is compatible with the systems used in Belgium (these include Cirrus, Maestro, Plus and Star). And make sure you know your PIN number.

4 Credit and Debit Cards

Most major credit and debit cards are accepted in Belgium. Restaurants almost always accept card payment, but check before you eat. A few of the smallest hotels accept only cash.

5 Travellers' Cheques

Travellers' cheques are becoming outdated, but they can be a useful back-up if your cards get lost or stolen, or fail to work. They can be exchanged for cash, or used as cash in certain circumstances.

6 Public Telephones

Mobile phones have made public pay-phones virtually redundant – but they still exist, operated by the former state company Belgacom, and can be used to make calls abroad. Public telephones operate with coins, or with Belgacom cards purchased from newsagents, ticket offices and post offices.

7 Post Offices

Post offices are generally open Mon–Fri 9am–5pm. You can buy stamps there and ascertain postage rates for heavier items. Main post offices have poste restante facilities, and some offer fax services. Stamps are also available from some tobacconists, newsagents and shops selling postcards.

8 Internet

Many of the more business-oriented and up-market hotels have Internet facilities. All the cities have cybercafés, but options are shrinking due to the wide availability of free Wi-Fi in hotels and restaurants.

9 Newspapers

The Belgian press is split across the language divide. The main French-language papers are *Le Soir*, *La Libre Belgique* and *La Dernière Heure*; the Dutch-speakers have *Het Laatste Nieuws*, *De Standaard* and *De Morgen*. English-language newspapers are widely available at news stands and in bookshops. Brussels also has its own excellent English-language monthly magazine called *The Bulletin*, offering a round-up and analysis of local events, news stories and issues; *Brussels Unlimited* has copious listings pages.

10 Television

Like their news-papers, Belgian television is split across the language divide, but cable brings in a wide choice of channels from all over Europe and the USA. Almost all hotel rooms have televisions.

Telephone codes

Belgian country code
+ 32 (drop the first 0 of the area code)

City area codes
Antwerp: (0)3
Bruges: (0)50
Brussels: (0)2
Ghent: (0)9

Dialling from Belgium
Britain: 00 44
USA/Canada: 00 1

English is widely spoken in all four of the cities covered in this book.

Left **Pharmacy** Right **Police officer giving directions**

TOP 10 Security and Health

1 Emergencies

The Belgians have a well-developed sense of community spirit, so if you are unfortunate enough to face an emergency, the chances are that you will receive sympathetic and effective assistance. The emergency services are as efficient and reliable as any in Europe. ✆ *Police: 101 • Fire/accident/ambulance: 100*

2 Travel Insurance

Take out travel and health insurance when you book your trip. This will allow you to claim compensation if you have to cancel, are delayed, or lose your possessions. It also covers medical costs in case of illness or accident. British citizens can take advantage of reciprocal EU medical agreements as long as they carry a European Health Insurance Card (EHIC), under which 75 per cent of specified costs can be reclaimed. You usually have to pay for medical treatment in the first instance and reclaim costs later, so keep all your receipts.

3 Doctors

If you suffer an accident or illness, you might be treated by a GP, or at one of the city hospitals. Ask locally about how best to access these services; for example, hotels have lists of duty doctors.

4 Dentists

Belgian dentists are generally of a high standard. Ask locally about how to access the services of a duty dentist.

5 Hospitals

Belgium has a tradition of hospital care dating back to medieval times. Most hospitals have been rehoused in modern buildings located in spacious grounds in the suburbs and on the periphery of the cities. They rank among the best in Europe.

6 Pharmacies

Pharmacists are highly trained, and their shops are often models of clinical efficiency. To many Belgians, the pharmacist is the first port of call for treatment of minor ailments. But pharmacists know the limits of their jurisdiction, and will refer you to a doctor if necessary. Each commune has a rota of late-night pharmacies.

7 Breakdowns and Motoring Accidents

If you take your car to Belgium, make sure you have full breakdown cover. If you don't, recovery costs and, worse still, the repatriation of your vehicle, can cost a small fortune. Breakdown services are offered by the two main Belgian motoring organizations: Touring and VAB. ✆ *Touring: 070 34 47 77 www.touring.be • VAB: 070 344 666. www.vab.be*

8 Crime

Belgian cities are not notably dangerous or crime-ridden places, but there is a fair amount of pick-pocketing, theft, and even car-jacking. If you remain alert and exercise the same precautions as you would in any other western city, the chances are that you will come through unscathed. If you are the victim of a crime, report it to the police – within 24 hours in the case of theft – if you wish to claim insurance. Many police officers speak English, and you are likely to get a professional response.

9 Embassies

In extreme cases – for instance, if you feel you have been unfairly treated by the police – you might wish to contact your country's embassy. ✆ *UK: Avenue d'Auderghem 10, 1040 Brussels (Etterbeek). Map G4. 02 287 62 11 • US: Blvd du Régent 27, 1000 Brussels. Map E3. 02 811 40 00*

10 Identity

You are obliged by law to carry an identity document (for example, a passport) at all times. The police are entitled to ask you to produce this for inspection, but they cannot take it away from you.

Left **Hotel Métropole** Right **Radisson Blu Royal**

Top 10 Brussels Hotels: Top of the Range

1 Hotel Métropole

A landmark Brussels hotel with lavish *belle époque* reception and bar. Rooms are fresh and pretty coloured. Centrally located, not far from Place Ste-Catherine and St-Géry. *Place de Brouckère 31, 1000 BRU • Map C2 • 02 217 23 00 • www.metropolehotel.com • €€€€€*

2 Astoria

With its palatial lobby and spectacular public rooms, the Astoria looks 18th-century, but was built in 1909. It stands in the Upper Town, near the Royal Palace. Churchill and Eisenhower stayed here. The Astoria is currently closed for renovation so call ahead. *Rue Royale 103, 1000 BRU • Map D2 • 02 227 05 05 • €€€€€*

3 Amigo

Steps away from the Grand Place, this smart hotel occupies the site of a 16th-century prison. Rooms are decked out in rich Flemish fabrics and Tintin sketches grace the bathroom walls. *Rue de l'Amigo 1–3, 1000 BRU • Map B3 • 02 547 47 47 • www.hotelamigo.com • €€€€€*

4 Sofitel Brussels Le Louise

Don't be deterred by the fact that this is a chain hotel, Sofitel brought in revered designer Antoine Pinto to redefine this five-star hotel with a glamorous, eclectic vibe. Rooms are plush and the restaurant has a sunny terrace. *Avenue de la Toison d'Or 40, 1050 BRU (Ixelles) • Map C5 • 02 514 22 00 • www.accorhotels.com • €€€€*

5 Brussels Marriott Hotel

A Marriott with unique character, located near the Bourse and the Grand Place, ideal for business, shopping and leisure. *Rue Auguste Orts 3–7, 1000 BRU • Map B2 • 02 516 90 90 • www.marriott.com • €€€€*

6 Manos Premier

This privately owned five-star boutique hotel offers 50 rooms styled with period furniture, an on-site spa and a restaurant. Guests can also enjoy the peaceful private garden. Very calm yet close to the bustling Avenue Louise. *Chaussée de Charleroi 100–106, 1060 BRU • Map C6 • 02 537 96 82 • www.manospremier.com • €€€€€*

7 Royal Windsor

Equidistant from the Grand Place and the Musées Royaux des Beaux-Arts, this elegant and sumptuous hotel features a series of "Fashion Rooms" designed by Belgian fashion designers. *Rue Duquesnoy 5, 1000 BRU • Map C3 • 02 505 55 55 • www.royalwindsorbrussels.com • €€€€€*

8 Radisson Blu Royal

The foyer is breathtaking – a towering atrium, with tropical plants and fountains filling its base, and glass-fronted lifts rising into the firmament. Managed with stylish efficiency, the hotel has a renowned restaurant, the Sea Grill *(see p74)*. *Rue Fossé-aux-Loups 47, 1000 BRU • Map C2 • 02 219 28 28 • www.radissonblu.com • €€€€€*

9 The Hotel

This high-rise may not look much from the outside, but the inside is brimming with surprises, including contemporary decor and stunning views of the city from most rooms, as well as the top-floor sauna and gym. Excellent service. Convenient transport links. *Boulevard de Waterloo 38, 1000 BRU • Map C5 • 02 504 33 35 • www.thehotel-brussels.be • €€€*

10 The Dominican

This luxurious hotel on a quiet street cannot be beaten for location, right behind Théâtre Royal de la Monnaie and within walking distance of the Grand Place. Award-winning architects have created a private courtyard over which the rooms look, and a very sumptuous Grand Lounge. *Rue Léopold 9, 1000 BRU • Map C2 • 02 203 08 08 • www.thedominican.be • €€€€*

Le Plaza

Price Categories

For a standard, double room per night (with breakfast if included), taxes and extra charges.

€	under €60
€€	€60–€100
€€€	€100–€175
€€€€	€175–€250
€€€€€	over €250

Brussels: Hotels of Character

1 Le Dixseptième

There is no other place quite like this in Brussels: an utterly charming and fascinating small hotel in the late-17th-century residence of the Spanish ambassador. It has a number of suites – named after Belgian artists – ingeniously devised beneath the roof beams, and furnished with a mixture of antique charm and modern flair. *Rue de la Madeleine 25, 1000 BRU • Map C3 • 02 517 17 17 • www.ledixseptieme.be • €€€€*

2 Odette en Ville

An intimate eight-room boutique hotel found in a 1920s building. Rooms are decorated with calming greys and whites, and feature first-rate fixtures such as under-floor heating. Romantic restaurant with freshly-cut roses and open fire. *Rue de Châtelain 25, 1050 BRU (Ixelles) • Map C6 • 02 640 26 26 • www.chez-odette.com • €€€€*

3 Le Plaza

You feel a bit like a guest of Louis XVI in the palatial foyer and public rooms of this grand hotel, with its stucco, gilt, and lavish ceiling paintings. The rooms maintain the same high standard of spacious comfort. *Boulevard Adolphe Max 118–26, 1000 BRU • Map C1 • 02 278 01 00 • www.leplaza-brussels.be • €€€€*

4 Warwick Barsey Hotel

Located at the southern end of stylish Avenue Louise, this hotel was decorated by French designer Jacques Garcia in an opulent Edwardian style. The rooms exude a sense of luxurious, silky comfort. *Avenue Louise 381–3, 1050 BRU • 02 649 98 00 • www.warwickbarsey.com • €€€€€*

5 Meininger

Housed in a former brewery, this backpacker-style, carbon-neutral, three-star hotel has over 170 fun rooms. Family rooms are available too. *Quai du Hainaut 33, 1080 BRU • Map A2 • 030 666 36 100 • www.meininger-hotels.com • €€€*

6 Pantone Hotel

The world's first hotel to apply the standardized Pantone colour-matching system used by designers from every continent. White walls and bedding allow colourful accessories to shine. Rooms 801 and 802 have rooftop views of the Lower Town. *Place Loix 1, 1060 BRU (Saint-Gilles) • Map C6 • 02 541 48 98 • www.pantonehotel.com • €€€*

7 Vintage Hotel

A 1960s-styled boutique hotel close to fashionable Avenue Louise. Rooms feature bubble lamps and psychedelic wallpaper. The breakfast room turns into a respected wine bar at night. *Rue Dejoncker 45, 1060 BRU (Saint-Gilles) • Map C6 • 02 533 99 80 • www.vintagehotel.be • €€*

8 Hotel Bloom!

A bright, fresh, modern hotel; all-white rooms each with a fresco painted by a young European artist. Located behind the botanical gardens with easy access to the Gare du Nord and the city centre. *Rue Royale 250, 1210 BRU • Map E1 • 02 220 66 11 • www.hotelbloom.com • €€€*

9 Ibis Styles Brussels Louise

The once independently run The White Hotel is now part of the Ibis chain, but it retains its contemporary all-white theme and continues to showcase artwork of young Belgian designers. Bicycle and scooter hire available. *Avenue Louise 212, 1050 BRU • Map C6 • 02 644 29 20 • www.ibis.com • €€€*

10 Espérance

This 1930s Art Deco gem is hidden away near Place des Martyrs *(see p70)*. Most rooms are modern now, but Room 7 still retains its old splendour. The tavern/breakfast room has hardly changed and is a must for evening drinks. *Rue du Finistère 1–3, 1000 BRU • Map C1 • 02 219 10 28 • www.hotel-esperance.be • €€€*

Left **Thon Hotel EU** Right **Marivaux**

Top 10 Brussels Hotels: Business & Budget

1 Sofitel Brussels Europe
Elegant five-star hotel just a stone's throw from the European Parliament. Extras include 11 meeting rooms, a hammam, a fitness centre and an on-site chocolate shop for last-minute gifts. *Place Jourdan 1, 1040 BRU • Map G5 • 02 235 51 00 • www.accorhotels.com • €€€€€*

2 Silken Berlaymont
Close to the heart of European government, this eco-friendly hotel is favoured by diplomats, politicians and journalists. They make full use of its state-of-the-art communication systems, fitness centre, Turkish baths and sauna. *Boulevard Charlemagne 11–19, 1000 BRU • Map G3 • 02 231 09 09 • www.hoteles-silken.com • €€€€€*

3 Thon Hotel EU
The Thon offers functional, modern rooms, free Wi-Fi, conference rooms, a fitness centre, a restaurant, and even a shopping mall. *Rue de la Loi 75, 1040 BRU • Map F4 • 02 204 39 11 • www.thonhotels.com • €€€€*

4 Radisson Blu EU Hotel
A deluxe hotel with spacious designer bedrooms, premier meeting rooms and Willards bar/restaurant. *Rue d'Idalie 35, 1050 BRU • Map E5 • 02 626 81 11 • www.radissonblu.com • €€€€*

5 Marivaux
A simple but satisfactory business hotel with elegant, contemporary styled guest rooms and state-of-the-art meeting rooms. Relax in the cocktail bar or enjoy a fusion-cuisine meal in the brasserie. *Boulevard Adolphe Max 98, 1000 BRU • Map C1 • 02 227 03 00 • www.hotelmarivaux.be • €€€€*

6 Le Méridien Brussels
Calm, contemporary hotel just around the corner from the Grand Place. The bar and restaurant are light and refined, and it is the only hotel in Belgium to have TelePrescence multi-video conferencing. *Carrefour de l'Europe 3, 1000 BRU • 02 548 42 11 • www.lemeridienbrussels.com • €€€€*

7 The Progress Hotel
Friendly, small hotel close to the Botanical Gardens with functional black-and-white rooms. After a day of business meetings, guests can enjoy relaxing on massage chairs in the covered winter garden with its 100-year-old olive trees, or with a drink at the bar. Airport pickups and customized sightseeing tours can be arranged. *Rue du Progres 9, 1210 BRU • Map C1 • 02 205 17 00 • www.progresshotel.be • €€€*

8 Aqua Hotel
Crisp, clean, good-value hotel that is popular with businesspeople looking for something a bit different – a huge, blue Arne Quinze sculpture twists through the entire building. *Rue de Stassart 43, 1050 BRU (Ixelles) • Map D5 • 02 213 01 01 • www.aqua-hotel-brussels.com • €€€*

9 Aloft Brussels Schuman
Funky, affordable boutique-design hotel in the heart of the EU district. Instead of a restaurant, there is a 24-hour "food station" serving snacks, sandwiches, salads and treats, as well as drinks. A choice of breakfast options is also available. Other facilities include free Wi-Fi, a fitness centre and a lively bar. *Place Jean Rey, 1040 BRU • Map G4 • 02 800 08 88 • www.aloftbrussels.com • €€*

10 2GO4 Grand Place
Just off the Grand Place this is Brussels' only city-centre hostel. With options to suit all budgets, the range of rooms on offer includes multi-share rooms, singles and doubles, with or without private bathrooms. There are excellent kitchen facilities and free Internet acccess. *Rue de Haringstraat 6–8, 1000 BRU • Map C3 • 02 219 30 19 • www.2go4.be • €€*

Die Swaene

Price Categories

For a standard, double room per night (with breakfast if included), taxes and extra charges.

€	under €60
€€	€60–€100
€€€	€100–€175
€€€€	€175–€250
€€€€€	over €250

Top 10 Bruges Hotels: Luxury

1 Die Swaene

An opulent, romantic hotel with rooms in the 18th-century building and in the modern "pergola" overlooking the river. Amenities include a swimming pool, a gastronomic restaurant and the Kaffee Pergola brasserie. *Steenhouwersdijk 1 • Map L4 • 050 34 27 98 • www.dieswaene.be • €€€€*

2 Hotel de Orangerie

This delightful hotel in a 15th-century convent has a gorgeous panelled breakfast room and lounge with a terrace overlooking the canal. The hotel exudes character and charm. *Kartuizerinnenstraat 10 • Map K4 • 050 34 16 49 • www.hotelorangerie.be • €€€€*

3 De Tuilerieën

In a 15th-century nobleman's house overlooking the canal, this lavish hotel has hosted many a celebrity. Swimming pool, steam room and bar. *Dijver 7 • Map L4 • 050 34 36 91 • www.hoteltuilerieen.com • €€€€€*

4 The Pand Hotel

This boutique hotel, in a fine 18th-century town house, is the ideal place for a romantic getaway. It is beautifully decorated in a very comfortable, deeply upholstered style, with canopied beds. Close to the Burg in a pretty tree-lined street. *Pandreitje 16 • Map L4 • 050 34 06 66 • www.pandhotel.com • €€€€*

5 Kempinski Dukes' Palace

This former ducal palace has definitely earned its five stars thanks to the spa pool, art gallery and chapel. The Manuscript restaurant serves a great breakfast. The bar is not cheap, but locals seem to think it's worth it. *Prinsenhof 8 • Map K4 • 050 44 78 88 • www.kempinski.com • €€€€€*

6 Bonifacius

A superb boutique B&B in a 16th-century building overlooking the canal and Bonifacius Bridge. Each room is decorated individually with rich fabrics and authentic antiques, and features an en-suite granite bathroom with Jacuzzi bath. Bonifacius is located opposite the Michelin-starred Den Gouden Harynck *(see p92)*. *Groeninge 4 • Map K5 • 050 49 00 49 • www.bonifacius.be • €€€€€*

7 NH Brugge

Once a 17th-century monastery, this building retains some lovely features such as stained-glass windows, large fireplaces and wooden beams. Rooms are modern, but the Jan Breydel bar has old-world charm. *Boeveriestraat 2 • Map J5 • 050 44 97 11 • www.nh-hotels.com • €€€€*

8 De Castillion

Occupying a 17th-century bishop's residence in the west of the city, this comfortable hotel has imaginatively decorated bedrooms and bathrooms. The high standard of the rooms is matched by the hotel's sumptuous restaurant, Le Manoir Quatre Saisons. *Heilige Geeststraat 1 • Map K4 • 050 34 30 01 • www.castillion.be • €€€€*

9 Crowne Plaza Hotel

You could not get more central if you tried: the Crowne Plaza overlooks the Burg at the very heart of Bruges. A modern establishment, it also incorporates some historic remains: the excavated foundations of the medieval church of St Donatian. The hotel has an indoor swimming pool, the PlazaCafé and its own car park. *Burg 10 • Map L4 • 050 44 68 44 • www.ichotelsgroup.com • €€€€€*

10 De' Medici

This smart, modern hotel, overlooking the canal in the quieter, eastern part of town, is a member of the Golden Tulip group. It has Japanese and Italian restaurants, as well as a bar, a gym, a sauna and Turkish baths. *Potterierei 15 • Map L2 • 050 33 98 33 • www.hoteldemedici.com • €€€€*

Left **Navarra** Right **Jan Brito**

Top 10 Bruges Hotels: Mid-range

1 Navarra
The former trading house of the merchants of Navarre is now a hotel of unusual elegance sited to the north of the Markt. It offers a high standard of service and comfort, including a fitness centre, swimming pool and jazz bar. *Sint-Jakobsstraat 41 • Map K3 • 050 34 05 61 • www.hotelnavarra.com • €€€*

2 Adornes
The Adornes is set in a renovated set of 16th- to 18th-century mansions overlooking the canal in the quieter, eastern part of the city, yet within walking distance of the centre. The decor, with its exposed beams, has rustic charm. Guests have free use of bicycles. Small pets are allowed. Closed during January. *Sint-Annarei 26 • Map L3 • 050 34 13 36 • www.adornes.be • €€€*

3 Prinsenhof
This regular award winner is tucked away down a side street in the west of the city, in an area once occupied by the splendid palace of the dukes of Burgundy. Something of the dukes' grand style pervades the decor – on a smaller scale, of course. Each room is invidiually decorated and very comfortable. *Ontvangersstraat 9 • Map K4 • 050 34 26 90 • www.prinsenhof.be • €€€€*

4 Hotel Malleberg
This homely, tastefully-decorated hotel located in a townhouse is family run and close to the Markt. The hearty buffet breakfast is served in a vaulted-ceiling basement. Free Wi-Fi in the guest rooms and common areas. Room rates, with tickets to various attractions, can be arranged. *Hoogstraat 7 • Map L4 • 050 34 41 11 • www.malleberg.be • €€€*

5 Hotel Jacobs
This good-value and intimate hotel is located in the quiet Saint-Gillis neighbourhood. Run by the affable Gentile family, it offers clean, comfortable public areas and cosy bedrooms with free Wi-Fi. Within walking distance to the main shops, restaurants and museums. *Baliestraat 1 • Map L2 • 050 33 98 31 • www.hoteljacobs.com • €€*

6 Egmond
The Egmond feels like a world apart, set in its own little tree-shaded park next to the Minnewater, in the south of the town. The façades and manor-house style give it a neo-baronial air. *Minnewater 15 • Map K6 • 050 34 14 45 • www.egmond.be • €€€*

7 Martin's Brugge
A peaceful, modern hotel with minimalist rooms decorated in rich reds and purples. On-site Arthie's bistro is good and you will receive free Wi-Fi if you book online. *Oude Burg 5 • Map K4 • 050 44 51 11 • www.martins-hotels.com • €€€*

8 Heritage
A smart, comfortable hotel in a 19th-century mansion, located in the old merchant quarter to the north of the Markt. It boasts a spa and fitness room in the 14th-century cellar, and a sun deck on the roof. *Niklaas Desparsstraat 11 • Map K3 • 050 44 44 44 • www.hotel-heritage.com • €€€*

9 Park Hotel
The Park Hotel is well-run, with a charming plant-filled breakfast/lunchroom and functional rooms. It overlooks the Zand, the spacious market square to the west of the city, and is 10 minutes from the city centre. *Vrijdagmarkt 5 • Map J5 • 050 33 33 64 • www.parkhotel-brugge.be • €€€*

10 Jan Brito
Centrally located, between the Burg and the Koningin Astridpark, the Jan Brito occupies an attractive 16th-century building with a step-gabled, brick façade. The charming public rooms are decorated in Louis XVI style. There is a pretty garden. *Freren Fonteinstraat 1 • Map L4 • 050 33 06 01 • www.janbrito.com • €€€*

De Pauw

Price Categories

For a standard, double room per night (with breakfast if included), taxes and extra charges.	€ under €60
	€€ €60–€100
	€€€ €100–€175
	€€€€ €175–€250
	€€€€€ over €250

TOP 10 Bruges Hotels: Budget

1 Hotel Biskajer

This small 17-room hotel just north of the Markt may lack amenities but this makes it an affordable option. All rooms have en-suite bathrooms, and a buffet breakfst is included in the price. There is a smart breakfast room and a small, cosy bar stocked with local beers. *Biskajersplein 4 • Map L3 • 050 34 15 06 • www.hotelbiskajer.com • €€€*

2 Patritius

Given its prices, the Patritius occupies a surprisingly grand 19th-century mansion located to the north-east of the Markt. *Ridderstraat 11 • Map L3 • 050 33 84 54 • www.hotelpatritius.be • €€*

3 Ter Brughe

Just north of the Augustijnenrei canal in a charming web of old streets, this well-run hotel occupies a 16th-century house overlooking the canal. It boasts some impressive ancient wooden beams, especially in the breakfast room. *Oost Gistelhof 2 • Map K3 • 050 34 03 24 • www.hotelterbrughe.com • €€*

4 Ter Duinen

This small hotel may seem a little out of the way in the north of the city, but the centre of Bruges is only a 15-minute walk away. The well-presented rooms are double-glazed and air-conditioned. The public rooms are stylish and welcoming. *Langerei 52 • Map L2 • 050 33 04 37 • www.terduinenhotel.eu • €€€*

5 Lucca

The 18th-century Neo-Classical exterior conceals an even older interior, with a vaulted medieval cellar in which guests breakfast. This was once the lodge of the merchants of Lucca – with connections to Giovanni Arnolfini, the banker who features in Jan van Eyck's famous painting, *The Arnolfini Marriage*. The rooms are quaintly old-fashioned – a fact reflected in the attractive room price. *Naaldenstraat 30 • Map K3 • 050 34 20 67 • www.hotellucca.be • C*

6 Ter Reien

Fetchingly perched beside the canal a little to the east of the Burg. Ter Reien's rooms are clean and the double bedrooms have capsule bathrooms. Book the spacious Honeymoon or Courtyard rooms if possible. *Langestraat 1 • Map L3 • 050 34 91 00 • www.hotelterreien.be • €€*

7 De Pauw

This pretty, family-run hotel, with its weathered brick exterior draped with flowers, is located close to the old parish church of St Giles, in the quiet and historic northern part of town – but still just a 10-minute walk from the centre. The interior is styled like a private home, with a welcome to match. *Sint-Gilliskerkhof 8 • Map L2 • 050 33 71 18 • www.hoteldepauw.be • €€*

8 Passage

Interesting budget hotel with just 14 chintzy, slightly faded rooms. It also has an adjacent "youth hotel", with cheaper prices. It is attached to the equally alluring Gran Kaffee de Passage *(see p93)*. *Dweerstraat 26 • Map K4 • 050 34 02 32 • www.passagebruges.com • €*

9 Bauhaus Hotel

A popular, energetic and friendly hostel. Located in the east of the city, a 15-minute walk from the centre, it prides itself on its cheap accommodation and offers a 10 per cent reduction at its Sacré Coeur bar/restaurant. *Langestraat 135 (reception at 145) • Map M3 • 050 34 10 93 • www.bauhaus.be • €*

10 Charlie Rockets

Located 2-minutes' walk from the Burg is this party hostel above an American-style bar with pool tables and live music on Friday nights. No curfew. Free internet access. *Hoogstraat 19 • Map L4 • 050 33 06 60 • www.charlierockets.com • €*

Left **Hotel Harmony** Right **Monasterium Poortackere**

Top 10 Ghent Hotels

1 Ghent River Hotel

This functional, modern hotel has 77 rooms occupying a converted 16th-century house and 19th-century factory. It is located on the bank of the River Leie close to the lively Vrijdagmarkt. The breakfast room boasts stunning views of the city. Sauna cabin too. *Waaistraat 5 • Map Q1 • 09 266 10 10 • www.ghent-river-hotel.be • €€€€*

2 Hotel Harmony

A stylish, family-run hotel located in Patershol, the oldest quarter of Ghent. The hotel features a courtyard swimming pool and a series of upscale rooms facing the canal; all have roof terraces with views over the city. *Kraanlei 37 • Map Q1 • 09 324 26 80 • www.hotel-harmony.be • €€€*

3 NH Gent Belfort

This chain certainly knows how to deliver style and comfort. The Belfort has all the facilities of a hotel of this rank, including a fitness room and sauna, and is very centrally located, opposite the Stadhuis. *Hoogpoort 63 • Map Q2 • 09 233 33 31 • www.nh-hotels.com • €€€€€*

4 Hotel de Flandre

Tucked behind the Korenlei quayside, this stylish town house has retained plenty of period detail in its public areas while its bedrooms are calm and comfortable. *Poel 1–2 • Map P2 • 09 266 06 00 • www.hoteldeflandre.be • €€€*

5 Hotel Gravensteen

Sitting opposite the Castle of the Counts, this 49-room hotel has a wow-factor entrance, comfortable rooms, a cosy bar with a great selection of Belgian beers, sauna and fitness room. The breakfast buffet offers a great selection of hot and cold choices. Guests have access to a private car park and are permitted to bring small pets. *Jan Breydelstraat 35 • Map P1 • 09 225 11 50 • www.gravensteen.be • €€€*

6 Ibis Gent Centrum Kathedraal

Right in the centre of Ghent, overlooking Sint-Baafskathedraal, this is a well-run, modern and attractive member of the reliable Ibis chain. There are plenty of eateries to choose from nearby. The private paying car park has limited spaces. *Limburgstraat 2 • Map Q2 • 09 233 00 00 • www.accorhotels.com • €€€*

7 Hotel Onderbergen

A quality hotel with reasonable room rates, located just a 3-minute walk from Sint-Baafskathedraal. Rooms are spacious with fun hand-painted design wallpaper. Guests are given a key for private access via the back door. *Onderbergen 69 • Map P3 • 09 223 62 00 • www.hotelonderbergen.be • €€€*

8 Monasterium Poortackere

Here is an interesting experience: a hotel in a converted convent. An air of tranquillity pervades the (largely 19th-century) buildings and grounds. A special place, enhanced by a warm welcome and a relaxed atmosphere – and a convenient location just west of the city centre. *Oude Houtlei 58 • Map P2 • 09 269 22 10 • www.monasterium.be • €€*

9 Hostel 47

This high-spec, privately owned youth hostel offers nine rooms within walking distance of Ghent's historical centre. It has trendy, comfortable common areas with free Wi-Fi and there is no curfew for guests. Payments can be made in cash only. *Blekerijstraat 47 • Map R1 • 0478 71 28 27 • www.hostel47.com • €*

10 Limited-Co Hotel

Five simple, stylish en-suite rooms (including a suite and a loft space) are on offer at this small hotel above a health-food restaurant. *Hoogstraat 58-60 • Map N2 • 09 225 14 95 • www.limited.co.be • €€*

Julien

Price Categories

For a standard, double room per night (with breakfast if included), taxes and extra charges.		
	€	under €60
	€€	€60–€100
	€€€	€100–€175
	€€€€	€175–€250
	€€€€€	over €250

Top 10 Antwerp Hotels

1 Julien

A contemporary hotel with stylish interiors. Fashioned out of two town houses linked by a green patio, it is located between Meir, the main shopping area, and the cathedral. *Korte Nieuwstraat 24 • Map T2 • 03 229 06 00 • www.hotel-julien.com • €€€*

2 Hotel Rubens

A quiet, romantic option located just behind the Grote Markt. Spacious one-bedroom suites have separate living rooms and lovely views. There is an attractive terrace where guests can enjoy breakfast in warm weather. The hotel is suitable for business travellers too. *Oude Beurs 29 • Map T1 • 03 222 48 48 • www.hotelrubensantwerp.be • €€€*

3 Mercure Antwerpen Centrum Opera

Located just behind the Meir shopping street, this chain hotel is fresh, modern and efficient. Rooms are spacious and comfortable. There is a delicious breakfast buffet and a cosy bar with a good choice of wines. *Molenbergstraat 9-11 • Map U2 • 03 232 76 75 • www.accorhotels.com • €€€*

4 Matelote

This converted town house near the River Scheldt offers nine dazzlingly white rooms all with minimalist decor and modern facilities. Breakfast is taken in the neighbouring Gin-Fish restaurant, which used to be called De Matelote (hence the name). *Haarstraat 11A • Map T2 • 03 201 88 00 • www.hotel-matelote.be • €€€*

5 Theater Hotel

This modern hotel lies in a convenient location close to the Rubenshuis, and is a short walk from the cathedral via some of Antwerp's best shopping streets. *Arenbergstraat 30 • Map U2 • 03 203 54 10 • www.vhv-hotels.be • €€€€*

6 Firean

A highly respected family run hotel in a 1920s Art Deco mansion. Although located further out of the centre than other options, Firean's unique charm makes the journey worthwhile. Rooms are spacious and feature rich fabrics. *Karel Oomsstraat 6 • Map U3 • 03 237 02 60 • www.hotelfirean.com • €€€*

7 't Sandt

This hotel in an old patrician mansion has been elegantly kitted out in a style you might call "Neo-Rococo". All the suites, including the luxurious penthouse, are set around a courtyard garden. It lies just to the west of the cathedral, and close to the river. *Zand 17 • Map T2 • 03 232 93 90 • www.hotel-sandt.be • €€€*

8 Radisson Blu Astrid Hotel

This is a large and well-run hotel, close to the Centraal Station, east of the city centre. It offers extensive conference facilities, and is well suited to the business traveller. It has a fitness suite and swimming pool. *Koningin Astridplein 7 • Map V2 • 03 203 12 34 • www.radissonblu.com • €€€€*

9 Hotel Docklands

Located in the up-and-coming docklands a 15-minute walk north of the centre, this Best Western-owned hotel sports a black-and-white colour scheme in the rooms and public areas. There is a well-stocked breakfast buffet, but no other meals are available. However, there are plenty of dining options nearby. *Kempisch Dok Westkaai 84-90 • Map U1 • 03 231 07 26 • www.hoteldocklands.be • €€€*

10 Pulcinella

This is possibly the smartest youth hostel in Belgium, featuring a minimalist interior with a mix of two-, four- and six-bed rooms and a designer bar. It is accessible to disabled travellers and has no curfew. *Bogaardeplein 1 • Map T3 • 03 234 03 14 • www.vjh.be • €*

General Index

D

E

F

Acknowledgments

The Author
Antony Mason is the author of a number of guide books, including the Cadogan City Guides to *Bruges* and to *Brussels (with Bruges, Ghent and Antwerp)*. He is also the author of the volume on *The Belgians* in the humorous Xenophobe's Guides series – along with more than 50 other books on history, geography, exploration and art. He lives in London with his Belgian wife Myriam and their son Lawrence.

For their help, deeply appreciated, the author would like to thank: Dawn Page, Ilse Van Steen, Anousjka Schmidt, Jean-Pierre Drubbel, Anne De Meerleer, Joke Dieryckx and Frank Deijnckens.

Produced by DP Services, a division of Duncan Petersen Publishing Ltd, 31 Ceylon Road, London W14 0PY
Project Editor Chris Barstow
Designer Janis Utton
Picture Researcher Lily Sellar
Indexer Hilary Bird

Fact Checker Dan Colwell
Main Photographer Anthony Souter
Additional Photography Demetrio Carrasco, Paul Kenward, David Murray, Rough Guides/ Anthony Cassidy, Jules Selmes, Paul Tait
Illustrator chrisorr.com
Maps Dominic Beddow, Simonetta Giori (Draughtsman Ltd)

For Dorling Kindersley
Publisher Douglas Amrine
Senior Art Editor Kate Poole
Senior Cartographic Editor Casper Morris
DTP Jason Little
Production Bethan Blase
Additional Editorial Assistance Emma Anacootee, Nadia Bonomally, Dan Colwell, Anna Freiberger, Rhiannon Furbear, Camilla Gersh, Claire Jones, Jude Ledger, Carly Madden, Sam Merrell, Kate Molan, Adrian Mourby, Catherine Palmi, Susie Peachey, Marianne Petrou, Simon Ryder, Sands Publishing Solutions, Emma Thomson, Stuti, Tiwari, Sadie Smith, Conrad van Dyk

Picture Credits
Key: a-above; b-below/bottom; c-centre; f-far; l-left; r-right; t-top.
Works of art have been reproduced with the permission of the following copyright holders: *Les Masques Singuliers* (1892) James Ensor ©DACS London 2011 13cra; *The Domain of Arnheim* René Magritte ©ADAGP, Paris and DACS, London 2011 13cr; *Baigneuse* (1910) Léon Spilliaert ©DACS London 2011 15b, *Les Troncs Gris* Léon Spilliaert ©DACS, London 2011 34br; ©Hergé/Moulinsart 2003 21cb, 55bl; Sofa Kandissy ©Alessandro Medini 39b.

The publishers would like to thank the following individuals, companies and picture libraries for permission to reproduce their photographs:

AKG-IMAGES: Collection Schloss Ambras, Innsbruck/Erich Lessing, *Charles V* (1549) copy after Tizian 47cr; Museum der Bildenden Künste, Leipzig, *Die Grubenarbeiterrinnen* (1880) by Constantin Meunier 37cr; Kunsthistorisches Museum, Vienna/Erich Lessing, *Philippe III le Bon (the Good), Duke of Burgundy* (c.1500) after a lost original by Rogier van der Weyden (Roger de la Pasture). Antwerp Tourist Office: 53br, 53bl, 61cl, 64-5c, 102tr, 104tl, 104cr, 105bl, 105cr, 106tl, 106tr.

BCB: Daniel Fouss 20–21c, 21bl, 21tl, 45cl. BRIDGEMAN ART LIBRARY: Christies Images, London, *Self Portrait* by Peter Paul Rubens (1557-1640) 30-31c; Koninklijk Museum voor Schone Kunsten, Antwerp, *Pièta* (c.1629) by Sir Anthony van Dyck 37tl.

CAFÉ DU VAUDEVILLE: Jean Mart 72tr. CH. BASTIN & J. EVRARD: 34tl, 44bc. CITY OF BRUSSELS MUSEUM/MAISON DU ROI: *The River Senne* by J.B. van Moer 11b. CORBIS: 56tr; Archivo Iconografico, S.A, *The Ghent Altarpiece* (1432) by Hubert van Eyck and Jan van Eyck (detail) 7crb, 36tr, 94tl, 26cb, 26br, 26-27c, 27cr, 27cb, 35br; Dave Bartruff 22cb; Michael Busselle 82-83c; Owen Franken 55cr; E.O. Hoppé 61cr; Tomas van Houtryve/VII 108tl; Diego Lezama Orezzoli 32-33c; Sygma/John Hasselt 50tr; Sygma/Van Parys 48clb.

DEN DIJVER: 92tr. DE VLAAMSE OPERA, GHENT: Kurt Van der Elst 60tr.

GETTY IMAGES: Hulton Archive/Apic 15bl. GHENT TOURIST OFFICE: 26tl, 94tr, 95tr, 96cl, 97cr.

HET BRUGS DIAMANTMUSEUM: 88tr. HOTEL HARMONY: Bram Declercq 130tl. HOTEL JULIEN: 131tl. HOTEL MARIVAUX:

126tr. HUISBROUWERIJ DE HALVE MAAN: 88tr.

IN FLANDERS FIELDS MUSEUM: 63tr.

KONINKLIJK MUSEUM VOOR SCHONE KUNSTEN, Antwerpen (België) 102tl.

LE CHÂTELAIN ALL SUITE HOTEL: Harshad B.ICKX 126tl.

Mtub 2003: J. Lafont 40tr, 78tl. MARTIN'S ORANGERIE: 127t.l MARY EVANS PICTURE LIBRARY: 47cl. MUSÉE D'IXELLES, BRUXELLES: Collection Ministère de la Communauté Française de Belgique, *Les Troncs Gris* by Léon Spillaert 34br ©DACS, London 2011. MUSÉE DES INSTRUMENTS DE MUSIQUE: 6cb, 16cla, 16-17c, 17t, 17cb, 17b, 38tr, 53tr. MUSÉE HORTA, BRUSSELS: *La Ronde des Heures* by Philippe Wolfers, photo Paul Luois 19cra. MUSÉE DES SCIENCES NATURELLES: Photo-foto irscnb-kbin Th.Hubin 41br. MUSÉES ROYAUX DES BEAUX-ARTS DE BELGIQUE BRUXELLES – KONINKLIJKE MUSEA VOOR SCHONE KUNSTEN VAN BELGIË: 14tr; photo J. Geleyns/www.roscan.be/ Portrait of Antony of Burgundy by Van der Weyden 13clb, /The King Drinks by Jacques Jordaens 34cl, /The Martyrdom of St. Sebastian by Hans Memling 13bc, photo Spoltdoorn, *Death of Marat* (1793) by Jacque-Louis David 6cl, 13tc, *Les Masques Singuliers* (1892) James Ensor ©DACS, London 2008 13cra, *Pietà* by Rogier van der Weyden 12bra, *The Domain of Arnheim* by René Magritte 13cr ©ADAGP, Paris and DACS, London 2011, *La Belle Captive* (1965) by Magritte 14tc; *Le Ruisseau* by Léon Frédéric (1856–1940) 15tr, *Portrait de Laurent Froimont* by Rogier van der Weyden 36bl, Triptyque: *Le Ruisseau* by Baron Léon Frederic 67bc; photo Cussac, *Episode des Journées de Septembre 1830 sur la Place de l'Hôtel de Ville de Bruxelles* (1835) by Baron Gustaf Wappers 46tr, *L'inhumation Precipité* by Antoine Wiertz 40bl, *L'assomption de la Vierge* by Peter Paul Rubens 36tl, *La Chute d'Icare* by Pieter Bruegel I 12bc. MUSÉE DAVID ET ALICE VAN BUUREN: 34tr. MUSEUMS AND HERITAGE ANTWERP: Sarah Blee 103br.

NEIL SETCHFIELD: 4-5c, 58tl.

OFFICE DE PROMOTION DU TOURISME WALLONIE: 76tl, 76cr.

RESTAURANT DE KARMELIET: 92tl. REX FEATURES: 48tr, 50cl, 51bl, 51cr; Sipa Press 48tl, 49tl. ROBERT HARDING PICTURE LIBRARY: 35tr; K. Gillham 87bl; Roy Rainford 88tl.

S.M.A.K.: Dirk Pauwels, Ghent 35cl. STEDELIJKE MUSEA BRUGGE: Groeningomuseum, *The Last Judgement* by Hieronymus Bosch 24c, *The Judgement of Cambyses* (1498) by Gerard David 24br, *The Virgin and Child with Canon van der Paele* by Jan van Eyck 25ca, Secret-Reflet (1902) Fernand Khnopff 25tr, *Portrait of Bruges Family* by Jacob van Oost the Elder 84tl; Memlingmuseum-Sint-Janshospitaal, *St Ursula Shrine* by Hans Memling 7ca, 24-5c, *The Adoration of the Magi* by Hans Memling 25cr, *The Moreel Triptych* by Hans Memling 25bl.

TAVERNE DU PASSAGE: 75tl TI ION HOTELS: 126tl. TOERISME BRUGGE/BRUGES TOURIST OFFICE: 07cr.

WORLD PICTURES: 62bl, Mike Hughes 56tl; Peter Scholey 6ca, 8-9c; Louise Thomson 85tr; Oliver Troisfontaines 86cl.

All other images © Dorling Kindersley. See www.DKimages.com for more information.

Phrase Book: French

In an Emergency

Help!	**Au secours!**	*oh sekoor*
Stop!	**Arrêtez!**	*aret-ay*
Call a doctor	**Appelez un medecin**	*apuh-lay uñ medsañ*
Call the police	**Appelez la police**	*apuh-lay lah pol-ees*
Call the fire brigade	**Appelez les pompiers**	*apuh-lay leh poñ-peeyay*
Where is the nearest telephone?	**Ou est le téléphone le plus proche**	*oo ay luh tehlehfon luh ploo prosh*

Communication Essentials

Yes/No	**Oui/Non**	*wee/noñ*
Please	**S'il vous plaît**	*seel voo play*
Thank you	**Merci**	*mer-see*
Excuse me	**Excusez-moi**	*exkoo-zay mwah*
Hello	**Bonjour**	*boñzhoor*
Goodbye	**Au revoir**	*oh ruh-vwar*
Good evening	**Bon soir**	*boñ-swar*
morning	**Le matin**	*matañ*
afternoon	**L'apres-midi**	*l'apreh-meedee*
evening	**Le soir**	*swah*
yesterday	**Hier**	*eeyehr*
today	**Aujourd'hui**	*oh-zhoor-dwee*
tomorrow	**Demain**	*duhmañ*
here	**Ici**	*ee-see*
there	**Là bas**	*lah bah*
What?	**Quel/quelle?**	*kel, kel*
When?	**Quand?**	*koñ*
Why?	**Pourquoi?**	*poor-kwah*
Where?	**Où?**	*oo*

Useful Phrases

How do you do?	**Comment allez vous?**	*kom-moñ talay voo*
Very well, thank you	**Très bien, merci**	*treh byañ, mer-see*
How are you?	**Comment ça va?**	*kom-moñ sah vah*
See you soon	**A bientôt**	*ah byañ-toh*
That's fine	**Ça va bien**	*sah vah byañ*
Where is/are …?	**Où est/sont …?**	*ooh ay/soñ*
Which way to …?	**Quelle est la direction pour …?**	*kel ay lah deer-ek-syoñ poor*
Do you speak English?	**Parlez-vous Anglais?**	*par-lay voo oñg-lay?*
I don't understand	**Je ne comprends pas**	*zhuh nuh kom-proñ pah*
I'm sorry	**Excusez-moi**	*exkoo-zay mwah*

Shopping

How much?	**C'est combien?**	*say kom-byañ*
I would like …	**Je voudrais**	*zhuh voo-dray*
Do you have …?	**Est-ce que vous avez …?**	*es-kuh voo zavay*
Do you take credit cards?	**Est-ce que vous acceptez les cartes de crédit?**	*es-kuh voo zaksept-ay leh kart duh kreh-dee*
What time do you open/close?	**A quelle heure vous êtes ouvert/fermé?**	*ah kel urr voo zet oo-ver/fermay*
this one	**celui-ci**	*suhl-wee see*
that one	**celui-là**	*suhl-wee lah*
expensive	**cher**	*shehr*
cheap	**pas cher, bon marché**	*pah shehr, boñ mar-shay*
size (clothing)	**la taille**	*tye*
white	**blanc**	*bloñ*
black	**noir**	*nwahr*
red	**rouge**	*roozh*
yellow	**jaune**	*zhownh*
green	**vert**	*vehr*
blue	**bleu**	*bluh*

Types of Shop

bakery	**la boulangerie**	*booloñ-zhuree*
bank	**la banque**	*boñk*
bookshop	**la librairie**	*lee-brehree*
butcher	**la boucherie**	*boo-shehree*
cake shop	**la pâtisserie**	*patee-sree*
chemist	**la pharmacie**	*farmah-see*
chip shop/stand	**la friterie**	*free-tuh-ree*
chocolate shop	**le chocolatier**	*shok-oh-lah-tyeh*
delicatessen	**la charcuterie**	*shah-koo-tuh-ree*
department store	**le grand magasin**	*groñ maga-zañ*
fishmonger	**la poissonerie**	*pwasson-ree*
greengrocer	**le marchand de légumes**	*mar-shoñ duh lay-goom*
hairdresser	**le coiffeur**	*kwafuhr*
market	**le marché**	*marsh ay*
newsagent	**le magasin de journaux/tabac**	*maga-zañ duh zhoor-no/ta-bak*
post office	**le bureau de poste**	*boo-roh duh pohst pos-tah-leh*
shop	**le magasin**	*maga-zañ*
supermarket	**le supermarché**	*soo-pehr-marshay*
travel agency	**l'agence de voyage**	*azhons duh vwayazh*

Sightseeing

art gallery	**la galérie d'art**	*galer-ree dart*
bus station	**la gare routière**	*gahr roo-tee-yehr*
cathedral	**la cathédrale**	*katay-dral*
church	**l'église**	*aygleez*
closed on public	**fermeture jour ferié**	*fehrmeh-tur zhoor fehree-ay*
garden	**le jardin**	*zhah-dañ*
library	**la bibliothèque**	*beebleeo-tek*
museum	**le musée**	*moo-zay*
railway station	**la gare (SNCB)**	*gahr (es-en-say-bay)*
tourist office	**les informations**	*uñ-for-mah-syoñ*
town hall	**l'hôtel de ville**	*ohtel duh vil*
train	**le train**	*trañ*

Staying in a Hotel

Do you have a vacant room?	**est-ce que vous avez une chambre?**	*es-kuh voo zavay oon shambr*
double room	**la chambre à deux personnes**	*shambr ah duh per-son*
with double bed	**avec un grand lit**	*ah-vek uñ groñ lee*
twin room	**la chambre à deux lits**	*shambr ah duhlee*
single room	**la chambre à une personne**	*shambr ah oon pehr-son*
room with a bath	**la chambre avec salle de bain**	*shambr ah-vek sal duh bañ*
shower	**une douche**	*doosh*
I have a reservation	**J'ai fait une reservation**	*zhay fay oon ray-zehrva-syoñ*

Eating Out

Have you got a table?	**Avez vous une table libre?**	*avay-voo oon tahbl leebr*
I would like to reserve a table	**Je voudrais réserver une table**	*zhuh voo-dray rayzehr-vay oon tahbl*
The bill, please	**L'addition, s'il vous plait**	*l'adee-syoñ, seel voo play*
I am a vegetarian	**Je suis végétarien**	*zhuh swee vezhay-tehryañ*
waiter waitress	**Monsieur/ Mademoiselle**	*muh-syur/ mad uh mwah-zel*
menu	**le menu**	*men-oo*
wine list	**la carte des vins**	*lah kart-deh vañ*
glass	**verre**	*vehr*
bottle	**la bouteille**	*boo-tay*
knife	**le couteau**	*koo-toh*
fork	**la fourchette**	*for-shet*
spoon	**la cuillère**	*kwee-yehr*
breakfast	**le petit déjeuner**	*puh-tee day-zhuh-nay*
lunch	**le déjeuner**	*day-zhuh-nay*
dinner	**le dîner**	*dee-nay*
main course	**le grand plat**	*groñ plah*
starter	**l'hors d'oeuvres**	*or duhvr*
dessert	**le dessert**	*duh-zehrt*
dish of the day	**le plat du jour**	*plah doo joor*
bar	**le bar**	*bah*
cafe	**le café**	*ka-fay*
rare	**saignant**	*say-nyoñ*
medium	**à point**	*ah pwañ*
well done	**bien cuit**	*byañ kwee*

Menu Decoder

agneau	*ahyoh*	lamb
ail	*eye*	garlic
asperges	*ahs-pehrj*	asparagus
bar/loup de mer	*bah/loo duh mare*	bass
boeuf	*buhf*	beef
brochet	*brosh-ay*	pike
café	*kah-fay*	coffee
café au lait	*kah-fay oh lay*	white coffee
caffe latte	*kah-fay lat-uh*	milky coffee
canard	*kanar*	duck
cerf/chevreuil	*surf/shev-roy*	venison
chicon	*shee-koñ*	Belgian endive
chocolat chaud	*shok-oh-lah shoh*	hot chocolate
choux de bruxelles	*shoo duh broocksell*	Brussels sprouts
coquille Saint-Jacques	*kok-eel sañ jak*	scallop
crêpe	*crayp*	pancake
crevette	*kreh-vet*	prawn
dorade	*doh-rad*	sea bream
epinard	*aypeenar*	spinach
faisant	*feh-zoñ*	pheasant
frites	*freet*	chips/fries
fruits	*frwee*	fruit
gauffre	*gohfr*	waffle
hareng	*ah-roñ*	herring
haricots	*arrykoh*	haricot beans
haricots verts	*arrykoh vehr*	green beans
homard	*oh-ma*	lobster
huitre	*weetr*	oyster
jus d'orange	*zhoo doh-ronj*	orange juice
l'eau	*oh*	water
le vin	*vañ*	wine
légumes	*lay-goom*	vegetables
limonade	*lee-moh-nad*	lemonade
lotte	*lot*	monkfish
moule	*mool*	mussel
poisson	*pwah-ssoñ*	fish
pommes de terre	*pom-duh tehr*	potatoes
porc	*por*	pork
poulet	*poo-lay*	chicken
raie	*ray*	skate
saumon	*soh-moñ*	salmon
thé	*tay*	tea
thon	*toñ*	tuna
truffe	*troof*	truffle
truite	*trweet*	trout
une bière	*byehr*	beer
veau	*voh*	veal
viande	*vee-yand*	meat
vin maison	*vañ may-sañ*	house wine

Numbers

0	**zéro**	*zeh-roh*
1	**un**	*uñ, oon*
2	**deux**	*duh*
3	**trois**	*trwah*
4	**quatre**	*katr*
5	**cinq**	*sañk*
6	**six**	*sees*
7	**sept**	*set*
8	**huit**	*weet*
9	**neuf**	*nerf*
10	**dix**	*dees*
11	**onze**	*oñz*
12	**douze**	*dooz*
13	**treize**	*trehz*
14	**quatorze**	*katorz*
15	**quinze**	*kañz*
16	**seize**	*sehz*
17	**dix-sept**	*dees-set*
18	**dix-huit**	*dees-zweet*
19	**dix-neuf**	*dees-znerf*
20	**vingt**	*vañ*
21	**vingt-et-un**	*vañ ay uhn*
30	**trente**	*tront*
40	**quarante**	*karoñt*
50	**cinquante**	*sañkoñt*
60	**soixante**	*swahsoñt*
70	**septante**	*setoñt*
80	**quatre-vingt**	*katr-vañ*
90	**quatre-vingt dix/ nonante**	*katr vañ dees/ nonañ*
100	**cent**	*soñ*
1000	**mille**	*meel*
1,000,000	**million**	*miyoñ*

Time

What is the time?	**Quelle heure est-il?**	*kel uhr eh-til*
one minute	**une minute**	*oon mee-noot*
one hour	**une heure**	*oon uhr*
half an hour	**une demi-heure**	*oon duh-mee uhr*
half past one	**une heure et demi**	*uhr ay duh-mee*
a day	**un jour**	*zhuhr*
a week	**une semaine**	*suh-men*
a month	**un mois**	*mwah*
a year	**une année**	*annay*
Monday	**lundi**	*luñ-dee*
Tuesday	**mardi**	*mah-dee*
Wednesday	**mercredi**	*mehrkruh-dee*
Thursday	**jeudi**	*zhuh-dee*
Friday	**vendredi**	*voñdruh-dee*
Saturday	**samedi**	*sam-dee*
Sunday	**dimanche**	*dee-moñsh*

Phrase Book: Dutch

In an Emergency

Help!	**Help!**	*help*
Stop!	**Stop!**	*stop*
Call a doctor!	**Haal een dokter!**	*Haal uhndok-tur*
Call the police!	**Roep de politie!**	*Roop duh poe-leet-see*
Call the fire brigade!	**Roep de brandweer!**	*Roop duh brahnt-vheer*
Where is the nearest telephone?	**Waar ist de dichtsbijzijnde telefoon?**	*Vhaar iss duh dikst-baiy-zaiyn duh tay-luh-foan*
Where is the nearest hospital?	**Waar ist het dichtsbijzijnde ziekenhuis**	*Vhaar iss het dikst-baiy-zaiyn -duh zee-kuh-hows*

Communication Essentials

Yes	**Ja**	*yaa*
No	**Nee**	*nay*
Please	**Alstublieft**	*ahls-tew-bleeft*
Thank you	**Dank u**	*dhank-ew*
Excuse me	**Pardon**	*pahr-don*
Hello	**Hallo**	*haa-lo*
Goodbye	**Dag**	*dahgh*
Good night	**Goedenacht**	*ghoot-e-naakt*
morning	**Morgen**	*mor-ghugh*
afternoon	**Middag**	*mid-dahgh*
evening	**Avond**	*av-vohnd*
yesterday	**Gisteren**	*ghis-tern*
today	**Vandaag**	*van-daagh*
tomorrow	**Morgen**	*mor-ghugh*
here	**Hier**	*heer*
there	**Daar**	*daar*
What?	**Wat?**	*vhat*
When?	**Wanneer?**	*vhan-eer*
Why?	**Waarom?**	*vhaar-om*
Where?	**Waar?**	*vhaar*
How?	**Hoe?**	*hoo*

Useful Phrases

How are you?	**Hoe gaat het ermee?**	*Hoo ghaat het er-may*
Very well, thank you	**Heel goed, dank u**	*Hayl ghoot, dhank ew*
How do you do?	**Hoe maakt u het?**	*Hoo maakt ew het*
See you soon	**Tot ziens**	*Tot zeens*
That's fine	**Prima**	*Pree-mah*
Where is/are ...?	**Waar is/zijn ...?**	*vhaar iss/zayn*
How far is it to ...?	**Hoe ver is het naar ...?**	*Hoo vehr iss het nar*
How do I get to ...?	**Hoe kom ik naar ...?**	*Hoo kom ik nar*
Do you speak English?	**Spreekt u engels?**	*Spraykt uw eng-uhls*
I don't understand	**Ik snap het niet**	*Ik snahp het neet*
Could you speak slowly?	**Kunt u langzamer praten?**	*Kuhnt ew lahng-zarmer-praat-tuh*
I'm sorry	**Sorry**	*sorry*

Shopping

I'm just looking	**Ik kijk alleen even**	*ik kaiyk alleyn ay-vuh*
How much does this cost?	**Hoeveel kost dit?**	*hoo-vayl kost dit*
What time do you open?	**Hoe laat gaat u open?**	*hoo laat ghaat ew opuh*
What time do you close?	**Hoe laat gaat u dicht?**	*hoo laat ghaat ew dikht*
I would like ...	**Ik wil graag ...**	*ik vhil ghraakh*
Do you have ...?	**Heeft u ...?**	*hayft ew*
Do you take credit cards?	**Neemt u credit cards aan?**	*naymt ew credit cards aan?*
Do you take travellers' cheques?	**Neemt u reischeques aan?**	*naymt ew raiys-sheks aan*
This one	**Deze**	*day-zuh*
That one	**Die**	*dee*
expensive	**duur**	*dewr*
cheap	**goedkoop**	*ghoot-koap*
size	**maat**	*maat*
white	**wit**	*vhit*
black	**zwart**	*zvhahrt*
red	**rood**	*roat*
yellow	**geel**	*ghayl*
green	**groen**	*ghroon*
blue	**blauw**	*blah-ew*

Types of Shop

antique shop	**antiekwinkel**	*ahn-teek-vhin-kul*
bakery	**bakkerij**	*bah-ker-aiy*
bank	**bank**	*bahnk*
bookshop	**boekwinkel**	*book-vhin-kul*
butcher	**slagerij**	*slaakh-er-aiy*
cake shop	**banketbakkerij**	*bahnk-et-bahk-er-aiy*
chip stop/stand	**patatzaak**	*pah-taht-zak*
chemist/drugstore	**apotheek**	*ah-poe-taiyk*
delicatessen	**delicatessen**	*daylee-kah-tes-suh*
department store	**warenhuis**	*vhaah-uh-houws*
fishmonger	**viswinkel**	*viss-vhin-kul*
greengrocer	**groenteboer**	*ghroon-tuh-boor*
hairdresser	**kapper**	*kah-per*
market	**markt**	*mahrkt*
newsagent	**krantenwinkel**	*krahn-tuh-vhin-kul*
post office	**postkantoor**	*pohst-kahn-tor*
supermarket	**supermarkt**	*sew-per-mahrkt*
tobacconist	**sigarenwinkel**	*see-ghaa-ruh-vhin-kul*
travel agent	**reisburo**	*raiys-bew-roa*

Sightseeing

art gallery	**gallerie**	*ghaller-ee*
bus station	**busstation**	*buhs-stah-shown*
bus ticket	**kaartje**	*kaar-tyuh*
cathedral	**kathedraal**	*kah-tuh-draal*
church	**kerk**	*kehrk*
closed on public holidays	**op feestdagen gesloten**	*op fayst-daa-ghuh ghuh-slow-tuh*
day return	**dagretour**	*dahgh-ruh-tour*
garden	**tuin**	*touwn*
library	**bibliotheek**	*bee-bee-yo-tayk*
museum	**museum**	*mew-zay-um*
railway station	**station**	*stah-shown*
return ticket	**retourtje**	*ruh-tour-tyuh*
single journey	**enkeltje**	*eng-kuhl-tyuh*
tourist information	**dienst voor toerisme**	*deenst vor tor-ism*
town hall	**stadhuis**	*staht-houws*
train	**trein**	*traiyn*

Staying in a Hotel

double room with double bed	**een twees persoons-kamer met een twee persoonsbed**	*uhn tvhays per-soans-*ka-mer met uhn *tvhay per-soans beht*

single room	**eenpersoons-kamer**	*ayn-per-soans kaa-mer*
twin room	**een kamer met een lits-jumeaux**	*uhn kaa-mer met uhn lee-zjoo-moh*
room with a bath/shower	**kaamer met bad/ douche**	*kaa-mer met baht/doosh*
Do you have a vacant room?	**Zijn er nog kamers vrij?**	*zaiyn er nokh kaa-mers vray*
I have a reservation	**Ik heb gereserveerd**	*ik hehp ghuh-ray-sehr-veert*

Eating Out

Have you got a table?	**Is er een tafel vrij?**	*iss ehr uhn tah-fuhl vraiy*
I would like to reserve a table	**Ik wil een tafel reserveren**	*ik vhil uhn tah-fel ray sehr-veer-uh*
The bill, please	**Mag ik afrekenen**	*muhk ik ahf-ray-kuh-nuh*
I am a vegetarian	**Ik ben vegetariër**	*ik ben fay-ghuh-taahr-ee-er*
waitress/waiter	**serveerster/ober**	*sehr-veer-ster/oh-ber*
menu	**de kaart**	*duh kaahrt*
wine list	**de wijnkaart**	*duh vhaiyn-kart*
glass	**het glass**	*het ghlahss*
bottle	**de fles**	*duh fless*
knife	**het mes**	*het mess*
fork	**de vork**	*duh fork*
spoon	**de lepel**	*duh lay-pul*
breakfast	**het ontbijt**	*het ont-baiyt*
lunch	**de lunch**	*duh lernsh*
dinner	**het diner**	*het dee-nay*
main course	**het hoofdgerecht**	*het hoaft-ghuh-rekht*
starter, first course	**het voorgerecht**	*het vhor-ghuh-rekht*
dessert	**het nagerecht**	*het naa-ghuh-rekht*
dish of the day	**het dagmenu**	*het dahg-munh-ew*
bar	**het cafe**	*het kaa-fay*
café	**het eetcafe**	*het ayt-kaa-fay*
rare	**rare**	*"rare"*
medium	**medium**	*"medium"*
well done	**doorbakken**	*door-bah-kuh*

Menu Decoder

aardappels	*aard-uppuhls*	potatoes
asperges	*as-puhj*	asparagus
bier	*beeh*	beer
chocola	*sho-koh-laa*	hot chocolate
eend	*aynt*	duck
fazant	*fay-zanh*	pheasant
forel	*foh-ruhl*	trout
frietjes	*free-tyuhs*	Chips/fries
fruit/vruchten	*vroot/vrooh-tuh*	fruit
garnaal	*gar-nall*	prawn
groenten	*ghroon-tuh*	vegetables
haring	*haa-ring*	herring
kalfsvlees	*karfs-flayss*	veal
kip	*kip*	chicken
knoflook	*knoff-loak*	garlic
koffie	*coffee*	coffee
kreeft	*krayft*	lobster
lamsvlees	*lahms-flayss*	lamb
lotte/zeeduivel	*lot/seafuhdul*	monkfish
mineraalwater	*meener-aahl-vhaater*	mineral water
mossel	*moss-uhl*	mussel
oester	*ouhs-tuh*	oyster
pannekoek	*pah-nuh-kook*	pancake
pike	*snoek*	snook
princesbonen	*prins-ess-buh-nun*	green beans
ree (bok)	*ray*	venison
rog	*rog*	skate
rundvlees	*ruhnt-flayss*	beef
Sint Jacoboester/ Jacobsschelp	*sind-yakob-ouhs-tuh/ yakob-scuhlp*	scallop
snijbonen	*snee-buh-nun*	haricot beans
spinazie	*spin-a-jee*	spinach
spruitjes	*spruhr-tyuhs*	Brussels sprouts
thee	*tay*	tea
tonijn	*tuhn-een*	tuna
truffel	*truh-fuhl*	truffle
varkensvlees	*vahr-kuhns-flayss*	pork
verse jus	*vehr-suh zjhew*	fresh orange juice
vis	*fiss*	Fish
vlees	*flayss*	meat
wafel	*vaff-uhl*	waffle
water	*vhaa-ter*	water
wijn	*vhaiyn*	wine
witloof	*vit-lurf*	Belgian endive/chicory
zalm	*sahlm*	salmon
zeebars	*see-buhr*	bass
zeebrasem	*zee-brah-sum*	sea bream

Numbers

1	**een**	*ayn*
2	**twee**	*tvhay*
3	**drie**	*dree*
4	**vier**	*feer*
5	**vijf**	*faiyf*
6	**zes**	*zess*
7	**zeven**	*zay-vuh*
8	**acht**	*ahkht*
9	**negen**	*nay-guh*
10	**tien**	*teen*
11	**elf**	*elf*
12	**twaalf**	*tvhaalf*
13	**dertien**	*dehr-teen*
14	**veertien**	*feer-teen*
15	**vijftien**	*faiyf-teen*
16	**zestien**	*zess-teen*
17	**zeventien**	*zayvuh-teen*
18	**achtien**	*ahkh-teen*
19	**negentien**	*nay-ghuh-tien*
20	**twintig**	*tvhin-tukh*
21	**eenentwintig**	*aynuh-tvhin-tukh*
30	**dertig**	*dehr-tukh*
40	**veertig**	*feer-tukh*
50	**vijftig**	*faiyf-tukh*
60	**zestig**	*zess-tukh*
70	**zeventig**	*zay-vuh-tukh*
80	**tachtig**	*tahkh-tukh*
90	**negentig**	*nayguh-tukh*
100	**honderd**	*hohn-durt*
1000	**duizend**	*douw-zuhnt*
1,000,000	**miljoen**	*mill-yoon*

Time

One minute	**een minuut**	*uhn meen-ewt*
one hour	**een uur**	*uhn ewr*
half an hour	**een half uur**	*een hahlf uhr*
half past one	**half twee**	*hahlf twee*
a day	**een dag**	*uhn dahgh*
a week	**een week**	*uhn vhayk*
a month	**een maand**	*uhn maant*
a year	**een jaar**	*uhn jaar*
Monday	**maandag**	*maan-dahgh*
Tuesday	**dinsdag**	*dins-dahgh*
Wednesday	**woensdag**	*vhoons-dahgh*
Thursday	**donderdag**	*donder-dahgh*
Friday	**vrijdag**	*vraiy-dahgh*
Saturday	**zaterdag**	*zaater-dahgh*
Sunday	**zondag**	*zon-dahgh*

Brussels: Selected Street Index